The NEW RULES *of* etiquette

*a young woman's guide to style and poise
at work, at home, and on the town*

Curtrise Garner

adamsmedia
Avon, Massachusetts

Published by
Adams Media, a division of F+W Media, Inc.
57 Littlefield Street, Avon, MA 02322. U.S.A.
www.adamsmedia.com

ISBN 10: 1-60550-006-2
ISBN 13: 978-1-60550-006-5

Printed in Canada.

J I H G F E D C B A

Library of Congress Cataloging-in-Publication Data
is available from the publisher.

This publication is designed to provide accurate and authoritative information with
regard to the subject matter covered. It is sold with the understanding that the publisher is not engaged in rendering legal, accounting, or other professional advice. If
legal advice or other expert assistance is required, the services of a competent professional person should be sought.

> —From a *Declaration of Principles* jointly adopted by a Committee of the
> American Bar Association and a Committee of Publishers and Associations

Many of the designations used by manufacturers and sellers to distinguish their prod-
uct are claimed as trademarks. Where those designations appear in this book and
Adams Media was aware of a trademark claim, the designations have been printed
with initial capital letters.

Interior illustrations by Eric Andrews.

This book is available at quantity discounts for bulk purchases.
For information, please call 1-800-289-0963.

I dedicate this book to the late Curtis Lee Garner.
Daddy, you knew I would be a writer long before I penned my first article.
Thank you for your guidance and support.

contents

INTRODUCTION   vii

CHAPTER 1

dining like a lady 1

CHAPTER 2

wine class 101 23

CHAPTER 3

tips on tipping 39

CHAPTER 4

introductions and mingling 53

CHAPTER 5

eating tricky foods 67

CHAPTER 6

parties and entertaining 87

CHAPTER 7

wedding decorum............................III

CHAPTER 8

baby showers...............................135

CHAPTER 9

the art of gift-giving.........................147

CHAPTER 10

social grace in the workplace..................157

CHAPTER 11

technology and etiquette 171

CHAPTER 12

the perfect host, the perfect guest 185

CHAPTER 13

tact during sad times 201

CONCLUSION 214
INDEX 215

introduction

When the first edition of Emily Post's *Etiquette* was published in 1922, the content focused on issues like whether or not to wear white after Labor Day. Ladies, we've come a long way.

Etiquette is not a topic limited to the dinner table or your wardrobe. From greeting your interviewer to comforting a friend who's suffered a loss, etiquette is associated with everything we do.

The New Rules of Etiquette is a comprehensive guide for today's young woman. Ranging from work to nights out with friends, this book offers you advice and guidance for the stickiest of situations.

In each chapter, you'll find a fictional vignette. You will meet Meagan, Cal, and Anissa—three young professionals looking to make their way to the top (without stepping on any toes) while still remaining supportive friends.

After the fictional faux pas, you'll find accessible and sensible advice. No matter what etiquette question you have, you'll find the answer in this complete guide for today's modern woman.

dining like a lady

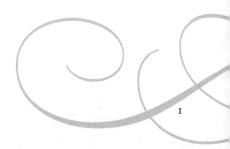

For the first time in forever, I am really, really excited about my job. After months of campaigning to my boss, Deanna, she finally selected me to pitch a new ad campaign to Extraordinaire Cosmetics, a potential client. Of course, landing a seven-figure client takes research, phone calls, follow-up e-mails, meetings, and more. The culmination of all my hard work was a business dinner at a swanky restaurant downtown. With accounting numbers and some preliminary PR and advertising strategies tucked into my bag, I hit the road—ready to wow them.

After I arrived at the restaurant and made my way to the table, I started to chat with Fred Buchanan, the Vice President of Marketing, before placing our dinner orders. My heart was pounding in my ears as I waited for a cue to start pitching the company's attributes and assets. Halfway through our meal, there was a lull in conversation and I knew it was now or never. Taking a deep breath and a sip from my glass of tea, I opened my mouth to start my pitch. Before I can get a word out, Fred snapped, "Meagan, you just drank from *my* glass!"

I felt like a deer in headlights, so I did the only think I could think of: I cracked a corny joke.

"I wanted to see if your tea was better than mine!" We both laughed but inside I was praying that my snafu wouldn't cost my company their business. That's all I need—for my lack of etiquette to be one more thing for Deanna to bang over my head.

After our meeting, I made a beeline to my favorite bar to meet up with my two best friends, Cal and Anissa.

When I arrive, they both have started without me. Cal is drinking a glass of Chardonnay. Practical, like her. Anissa is drinking something exotic—pink on the top and clear on the bottom. Complex, like her.

"So, what happened, dear?" asks Cal, who is all ears.

"I think I bombed the pitch to Extraordinaire Cosmetics! I made a mistake and drank out of the client's glass and he noticed. Can you imagine that! A guy who actually knows more etiquette than I do!"

"He probably won't even remember that you drank out of the wrong glass," Anissa offers, trying to make me feel better. "I mean, look at you. You look absolutely flawless! I bet that's what he'll remember."

I certainly hoped so. Deanna was really hard to please and I wanted to show her I could reel in this account. I crossed my fingers and ordered a shot. ❧

Some of us were raised where dining in restaurants was the norm and thus know the basics: Keep your elbows off the table; don't eat with your hands, and never, ever snap your fingers to get your waiter's attention. Still, after entering the professional world, there is more to learn than not to speak with your mouth full. Regardless of your dining history, certainly you know that there's a lot more to enjoying a meal at a restaurant—especially when it comes to an upscale eatery with countless pieces of silverware, several glasses, and fingerbowls. This type of dining is a far cry from eating at your parents' where the only rules are that you sit up straight in your chair and never complain about your mother's meatloaf recipe.

Who's Footing the Bill?

Proper etiquette surrounding restaurant dining begins even before you hand your car keys to the valet.

If you are hosting a get-together at a restaurant or wining and dining business contacts, you should make the reservation and plan on picking up the check. If the occasion is more informal and you don't plan on buying everyone's dinner, you should make it clear that each party is responsible for his or her own meal—before the actual date. A tactful way to do this? When inviting your guests, say something like, "I wanted to try the new restaurant in town. The menu prices are around $20 for a dinner, not including the specials. Do you think you'd like to go?" By mentioning the prices on the menu, your friend will know that you are expecting her to pay her own way. Or, if there is any question, it gives your friend the opportunity to ask if she should prepare to pay for her own meal.

If you are hosting the group, make arrangements in advance to pay the bill. Never hassle with your guests over the check. However, if one of your guests tries to grab the bill at a dinner you're hosting, it can quickly become uncomfortable for you, your guest, and the server. First, try reminding your guest that you extended the invitation to dinner and are happy to pay. If your guest insists, try to minimize the situation. While you may be less than comfortable with someone else picking up the tab, perhaps you can offer to split the check so that your friend, coworker, or business contact is not stuck with the entire bill.

Dealing with the check is not the only tricky aspect to restaurant dining. Read on for how to handle late arrivals, order your meal politely, and less-than-satisfactory meals.

The Fine Details of Fine Dining

If you are the first person to arrive at a restaurant, you may wait for the host or ask to be seated at the reserved table. This is the easy part. After that, there are many possibilities for committing a faux pas.

Arriving Late

Once seated, if you are the host, it is polite to wait fifteen minutes for all of the guests to arrive before placing orders and beginning the meal. The host and the guests that are present can order drinks and hors d'oeuvres while waiting for the complete party. After that, rather than keep your other guests waiting, you can begin to order your meals.

If you are a guest who is running late, call the restaurant and leave a message for the host or hostess stating that you will be late, and estimate the time you expect to arrive. Since the host is waiting for you, she might check her cell phone before putting it away while dining. In that case, you can call the host and speak briefly or send a text message—if you are not driving. However, if you realize that your arrival will take longer than expected, you can always ask one of the guests to order your meal. If you show up later than fifteen minutes, expect that the other guests will have already placed their orders. In the event that something happens and you are unable to attend the dinner, you should reimburse the person who paid for your meal as soon as possible.

At the Table

When settling in at the table, wait for the host or guest of honor to pick up the napkin and place it on his or her lap—and then do the same. If you need to use your napkin prior to the beginning of the meal, try to do so without calling attention to yourself. After using the napkin, fold it neatly and place it to the left of your plate. Place it on your lap after the host begins the meal.

This type of dining is a far
cry from eating at your
parents' house.

- A dinner napkin is placed on the lap folded in half. A luncheon-sized napkin can be opened all the way. In upscale restaurants, your waiter will place the napkin on your lap for you.
- Your napkin will be placed either to the left of the forks, beneath the forks, or on the main plate in a decorative fashion
- Never flap your napkin before placing it in your lap, and neither men nor women should tuck the napkin in the shirt like a bib.
- Never use your napkin to wipe off lipstick or blow your nose. The purpose of the napkin is to dab at the corners of your mouth.
- If you leave the table during a meal, place your napkin on your chair. When you have finished dining, place your loosely folded napkin (so that the server knows it has been used) to either the right or left of your plate. Never place the napkin back in the napkin ring.

Placing Your Order

A conscientious waiter will wait for diners to close their menus as a sign to take orders. If the waiter appears before everyone is ready to order, the host should ask for a few more minutes for his or her guests.

The server, or in some cases the maitre d', will take your order for cocktails before your meal. Depending on the length of the dinner, you may order your appetizer or salad before your meal, or you may order it at the same time. Either way, you can expect your server to stagger the arrival of the two courses.

The person on the right of the host or hostess should order first. If you have not decided on your selection when it's your turn to order, ask for another moment. As a guest, do not order the most expensive item on the menu—even if the meal is a business expense.

You may ask the server about dishes with which you are unfamiliar. Also, you may ask about the price of the specials that do not appear on the menu. Typically, specials are presented at fine-dining establishments. However, if the cost of an item is not listed on the menu or mentioned by the server, you can ask the price at any restaurant.

When eating with a group, it's perfectly fine to start eating hot food when it is served—don't wait for everyone to begin. However, if your host waits until everyone is served then you should do the same. When eating cold food, wait for everyone to be served.

anissa says ...

Try to remember that some foods (spaghetti, artichokes, and shellfish) are more difficult to eat than others. Keep this in mind when dining formally.

If your food is cooked improperly, or if you are served the wrong dish, quietly bring it to the attention of your server and wait for them to bring you another plate. Under no circumstances should you yell, curse, or file a complaint. If the second meal is not prepared to your satisfaction, then you can ask to speak to the manager of the restaurant and discreetly file a complaint. Encourage the other diners at the table to continue with their meals since it might take a few minutes before your new serving arrives. If your food arrives at the end of the meal—which the waiter will certainly try to prevent—you can ask for a doggy bag. There is no need to apologize to the other diners for returning your meal.

If you drop a utensil on the floor, never lean over to pick it up. Simply beckon the waiter and ask for another. The waiter will pick up the utensil and bring you a clean one.

Selecting Wine

Typically, the host selects the wine, although a host may pass the wine list around the table for others to review, or ask a guest to select a wine.

A rule of thumb is to spend as much on one bottle of wine as you spend on one complete, individual dinner. If you are hosting several people, the host can order a red and a white wine to complement everyone's meal. Ordering a red and a white wine fits most palates and should pair well with various meals. The host also can ask guests what type of wine they prefer or suggest a red wine if everyone is eating hearty entrées. Likewise, if everyone is enjoying seafood, then suggest a white wine. If you find that the majority of the guests prefer a certain wine and one or two have a different preference, the host can order a bottle that suits the majority of the guests and the others can order an individual glass.

If you are uncertain of what wine to select, ask your server for a recommendation. If you use the services of a sommelier, tip this wine expert 15 percent of the cost of the wine in addition to the normal gratuity that you give to your server. You can discreetly hand the sommelier a cash tip or include the amount on the bill as part of the entire tip.

Coffee, Tea, and Desserts

When drinking coffee, tea, and other hot drinks, a saucer may be provided underneath the cup to put your teaspoon on. If there isn't a saucer, the spoon may be placed facedown on a place mat or on the edge of a butter plate or dinner plate. Do not drink from a mug with a spoon in it.

If coffee or tea spills on your saucer, it is acceptable to ask for a new saucer. If a saucer is not available, or it is inconvenient to ask for a new saucer, use paper napkins to absorb the spilled tea and let the napkin sit there. Tuck sugar wrappers under your saucer or next to your plate, lying flat, not crumpled. Leave butter wrappers or jelly containers on your butter plate.

cal says ...

When handling a cup and saucer, always hold the cup with one hand, by the handle, with your fingers in.

Never order more than one dessert. And, never sample a dessert from another person's plate. If you want to sample their dessert, ask your server for another dessert plate. Sometimes the dessert will be split in the kitchen if you tell the server that you intend to divide the dish.

Doggy Bags

Doggy bags are one of those things where any approach is acceptable. Some people have no problem taking a doggy bag home, regardless of how fine the dining experience. Others wouldn't dream of take a doggy bag under any circumstances. Both are correct. Whether or not to take a doggy bag is up to the diner. If you're at a restaurant and want to bring your leftovers home, you should feel free to do so.

COMMON *Table-Manner* MISTAKES

Keep elbows off the table. Your grandmother was right—do not rest your elbows on the table, even between bites. Place your hands in your lap if you need to rest them.

Do not interrupt when others are speaking. When someone is addressing you or asking a question, allow the other person to finish his thoughts (even if he is long-winded.) Then, respond to the person. This requires great listening skills—something many need to work on.

Do not pick your teeth at the table. Use your tongue to discreetly remove food. If this doesn't work, excuse yourself from the table and remove the food in the bathroom.

Do not blow your nose at the table. You may dab your nose discreetly if it is bothering you. If you need to blow your nose, excuse yourself and do so in the bathroom.

Do not snap your fingers to get a waiter's attention. Simply wait for your waiter to come into view, make eye contact, and discreetly beckon him or her. Once the waiter is at your table, you may then make your request known. *Never* snap your fingers, whistle, or clap your hands to get your waiter's attention.

Do not call the waiter "Miss," "Mrs," or "Mister." When addressing the waiter, you may use his or her name, if you know it, or you may say, "Waiter" or "Waitress."

COMMON *Table-Manner* MISTAKES

Do not apply makeup or comb your hair at the table. Excuse yourself and apply makeup and smooth hair in the powder room/bathroom before returning to the table.

Do not push food onto your fork or knife with fingers. Use your knife to push the food onto your fork or spear the food with your fork.

Do not place your purse on the back of your chair or on the table. Set it on the floor slightly under your chair so that the wait staff or others won't trip over it and where it won't be in the way.

Do not use the phone, take, or make calls at the table. Do not use your cell phone at the table—not even to send a text message. If you must take a phone call, quietly excuse yourself from the table and take your phone call. Return to the table when you are finished.

Do not push your plate away when you have finished eating. Rest your utensils across your plate so the server knows you have completed your course or meal. (See the end of this chapter for more information.)

Do not comment on food that you dislike or are allergic to when that food is served. Simply decline the food and say, "No, thank you."

Do not eat directly off someone's plate. If you are sharing a meal, always ask for two plates so that you can divide the food into separate portions and place your portion onto your plate. Nicer restaurants may do this for you in the kitchen before the item is brought to your table.

dining like a lady

13

What's What at the Table

At after-work happy hours or weekend lunches with your girlfriends, it's unlikely you have any trouble figuring out what's what in your place setting. A fork, one knife, one plate—it's not rocket science. However, at finer dining establishments, the display of silverware, glasses, and plates can be a land mine of etiquette mishaps. As you read earlier in the chapter, sipping from someone else's glass or using the incorrect fork can make you look uncouth. At a business dinner, a formal party—whatever the occasion—you want to look and feel like the refined lady you are. Not only will the information in this section help you dine out like a pro, it will also give you tips to set your table for formal dining at home.

Plates and Chargers

In a formal dining setting, a charger (sometimes called a service plate) is usually placed underneath the dinner plate. The charger is a decorative, oversize plate used to add color and pattern to the table setting.

The main dinner plate is found in the center of the place setting in front of each chair. The bread plate is always to the left, slightly above the forks, and has a small knife placed across the top, which is the butter spreader.

Chargers can be made of almost any material, including china, pewter or straw.

If you're entertaining at home, chargers can be a fun and easy way to enhance your dinner table. Never serve food directly on a charger, but you can set a first-course soup bowl or salad plate on top of it. Clear the charger from the table along with the bowl or plate. Once the charger is removed from the table, it is not used again.

Glasses

In a formal dining setting, glasses are everywhere! Don't let this throw you off. You just have to remember one rule and you'll be ready to go: use the glasses from right to left, or start with the glass furthest away and work your way toward your plate.

meagan says ...

Be sure to hold most stem glasses by the bowl, except for the white wine glass or the Champagne flute. The reason for this is to prevent you from warming the white wine and Champagne with your hand, since they are both served chilled.

Typically, you'll see a sherry glass, white wine glass, red wine glass, water glass, and Champagne flute. The glasses are placed on the table in this order (from outside in, or farthest to the right).

When entertaining at home and serving a variety of beverages, set each place with all the glasses that will be used during dinner (except dessert-wine glasses, which are brought out when dessert is served). Place the water glass to the right of the plate, just above the knives. Wineglasses are placed to the right of the water glasses in the order in which they will be used.

The next section is an overview of the glasses you will find at a fine dining establishment. If you are entertaining formally, you should have the following glasses on hand.

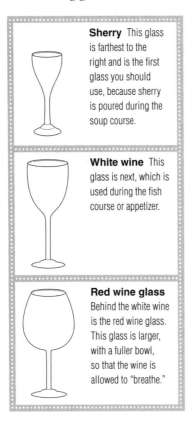

Sherry This glass is farthest to the right and is the first glass you should use, because sherry is poured during the soup course.

White wine This glass is next, which is used during the fish course or appetizer.

Red wine glass Behind the white wine is the red wine glass. This glass is larger, with a fuller bowl, so that the wine is allowed to "breathe."

Water goblet The water goblet is the largest glass and sits right above the dinner knife.

Champagne flute Behind and to the right of the water goblet is the Champagne flute. This is the last glass used at a formal setting, during dessert.

Silverware

In addition to multiple glasses on the table, silverware is also abundant. However, as with glasses, a proper silverware setting follows the same, simple rule: Use the silverware on the table in the order it will be used, from the outside in.

Forks are placed to the left of the plate, and knives and spoons to the right. The only exception is the cocktail fork, which is placed to the right of the soup spoon and used to eat seafood cocktails. The dessert fork and spoon are placed above the dinner plate.

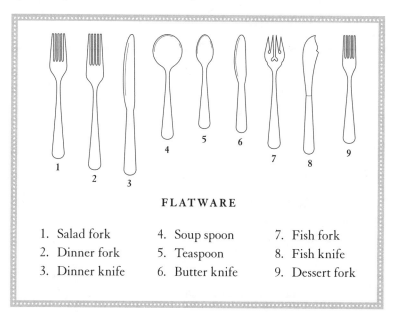

FLATWARE

1. Salad fork
2. Dinner fork
3. Dinner knife

4. Soup spoon
5. Teaspoon
6. Butter knife

7. Fish fork
8. Fish knife
9. Dessert fork

The salad fork, smaller than the dinner fork, is typically placed farthest to the left. This means that salad will be your first course. The one exception is if fish is being served as the first course, then the fish fork is to the left of the salad fork. However, when salad is served as a third or fourth course, the salad fork rests closest to the plate. Next to the salad fork is the dinner fork, which is used to eat your entrée. As mentioned earlier, the butter spreader is placed on your bread plate, on the left above the forks.

Now that we've covered the utensils on the table, it's time to dine.

Styles of Dining

There are two basic methods for cutting foods and using silverware at a meal: the European, or Continental style, and the American style. Both are acceptable, but it's important to use either one or the other—not both. Get ready to pick up your utensils (using the outermost utensils for your first course, naturally) and start digging in.

European Or Continental Style

When using the European or Continental style, (sometimes called the two-step cutting method), keep the fork in your left hand and use it to pierce the food and bring to your mouth. Raise the fork with the tines down, keeping your forearm toward your mouth. The knife stays in your hand, ready to be used again. If you need to maneuver food onto the times of the fork, use the knife to push the food on the knife.

EUROPEAN DINING

EUROPEAN REST

When resting between bites, cross the fork with the tines down across the knife. For the fork, visualize a clock, with the tines of the fork at the two and the handle facing the eight. For the knife, the tip of the knife faces the ten and the handle faces the four. This position will signify that you are not finished with your meal.

American Style

American style, which is only used in the United States and Canada, is sometimes called the zigzag. Using this method, hold the fork in your left hand, tines down to secure the food. Cut with the knife, holding the handle in the palm of your right hand. After you cut your food, lay the knife on your plate near the top and switch the fork to your right hand.

AMERICAN DINING

AMERICAN REST

The American method calls for placing a hand at rest in the lap when you are eating with only a fork or spoon. If you are left-handed, all of the above hand positions can be reversed.

When taking a break between bites while dining American style, place your knife and fork, with the handles to the right, on the plate. Never rest the handles on the table.

All Done!

If you're in a restaurant, the way you place your silverware on the plate can be a sign that you have completed your meal. You've probably had an overly attentive waiter whisk your plate away before you've finished dining. To avoid this, place your knife and fork side by side in the four o'clock position (or the ten-twenty position) with the blade of the knife facing in. Your server will know that you are finished and will remove your plate and serve the next course. Alternatively, you can crisscross the knife and fork over the other to signal that you are finished with your meal.

FINISHED

Technical Tools

While the previously mentioned silverware, flatware, and glasses are typically all you will find on a table when dining out, depending on the nature of the restaurant, you may also encounter some additional items. So how do you handle chopsticks, fingerbowls, and the like? Read on for easy tips to using these tools like a pro.

Using Chopsticks Like a Professional

Using chopsticks can be an intimidating prospect. However, it can be a fun and a culturally rich experience if you use them correctly.

The narrow end of the chopsticks always holds the food. Pick up one chopstick and hold it about one-third of the way from the top. Rest it between your thumb and fourth finger.

Pick up the second chopstick and rest it between your second and third fingers, using the thumb for support. Your second and third fingers control the movement of the top stick that is used to pick up and hold food.

To pick up food, hold the chopsticks so that the narrow ends act like pinchers. Grasp a piece of food with the chopsticks and guide it to the mouth. Most foods are eaten from the plate or bowl in this manner. When eating rice, the bowl may be picked up and the rice directed into the mouth using the chopsticks.

Place the chopsticks across your bowl or plate between bites or at the end of the meal. Do not rest chopsticks standing upright in your rice or soup bowl. Some Japanese restaurants provide a small ceramic piece on which to rest your chopsticks.

Do not be embarrassed to ask for help with your chopsticks. If you are more comfortable using a fork or a knife, it is acceptable to ask for one.

Sushi is fresh raw fish and vinegary rice, served in hand-shaped, bite-sized pieces so that you can easily eat it with chopsticks. You also can eat sushi with a fork, but many sushi lovers use their fingers. Regardless of the utensils you decide to use, you should eat sushi with one or two bites. Sushi is served with soy sauce and various condiments for dipping. Ginger is provided as a refresher for the palate between courses.

Finger Bowls

Finger bowls are presented after the main course and before dessert arrives. The bowls are a great help after eating finger foods such as barbeque, corn on the cob, shellfish, or any other handheld food. Your server places it in front of you on a plate, usually with a doily underneath the bowl. The bowl contains warm water with a slice of lemon and a small flower. A small dessert fork and spoon also are on the plate. Remove the utensils from the plate and place them to the left and right, respectively, of where the dessert plate will go.

Simply dip the fingers of one hand and then the other into the bowl, and wipe them with a napkin. Remove the doily and bowl and place them to the left. A waiter then removes them. Never drink the water.

While this may seem like a lot to remember, the most important thing to keep in mind while dining formally is to maintain an air of confidence. If you make a mistake and one of your fellow diners notices, excuse yourself and carry on without drawing too much attention to yourself. And when in doubt, you can always look to your host for a visual reminder of how to wine and dine like a professional.

CHAPTER 2

wine class 101

After a long week at work, I am ready to kick back. Tonight, Anissa is hosting a dinner party. Ever since she attended a holiday dinner at a coworker's house, she has wanted to do something similar—only better.

At the party, I am seated between Cal (who has brought her new man, Jimmy) and one of Anissa's coworkers, Whitney. After chatting for a bit, I realize that she is the same coworker who hosted the holiday party. Based on what Anissa has told me and the way she is making sure every detail is perfect, I deduce that while Whitney is Anissa's friend, she also is a friendly rival.

After clearing our salads, Anissa returns from the kitchen with a whole roasted chicken that looks like something right out of G. Garvin's kitchen. The room instantly fills with a heavenly aroma, and as everyone oohs and ahhs over the chicken, I wink at my friend to let her know how fabulously she's doing.

"Who's ready for more wine?" Anissa asks. We have been sipping Champagne, and while it's lovely, we're all ready to switch it up.

As we pass side dishes around, Anissa opens an expensive looking bottle of merlot.

Now I don't know much about wine, but I do know that merlot is notorious for being difficult to pair with food, and that white wine is usually better with poultry. Based on the skeptical look on Whitney's face, she knows it too.

As everyone begins eating dinner, I take a sip of my wine. Not a good match at all. While the food is cooked perfectly, the merlot is much too rich to be paired with a big meal. And to make matters worse, Whitney says, "This meal would have been better with a nice white wine."

Across the table, I lock eyes with Anissa who looks a little embarrassed and at the same time annoyed. However, only Anissa and I hear her. The rest of the guests are not letting a slightly clumsy wine pairing ruin their good time, but I know Anissa was really looking to knock it out of the park tonight. Oh well. At least the food was delicious. ❧

All ladies know the one true rule to drinking and enjoying wine: Simply drink what you like. To appreciate wine, all you really need are your eyes, nose, and mouth. Wine is meant to be enjoyed and you certainly want to taste several types—not all at the same time—to determine what you like.

Before getting into the nuances of wine, there are a few basics that everyone should know. First, the variety of grapes used in a wine determine the wine's color, aroma, and taste. The deeper the color and aroma, the more full-bodied the wine. Further, wine should always be clear without any cloudiness or haziness. Lack of clarity indicates a flaw in the wine-making process. There's one other rule to wine: Never, ever drink a flawed wine.

The Taste and Aroma of Wines

Sniffing and tasting wine is the really fun part of getting to know wine. To make sure your nose sniffs the whole body of the wine, always swirl the wine first. Then, stick your nose into the glass and sniff the various aromas.

To strengthen the nose and its skills for identifying smells, practice smelling all kinds of things, including vegetables, fruits, and flowers. This way, you'll be able to readily draw on those smells when smelling wines.

You'll often hear the terms *fruity*, *acidic*, *grassy*, and *dry* when someone is describing a wine. Whether it's your wine-loving next door neighbor or even the sommelier at a fine restaurant, it's nice to know exactly what they're talking about. If you want to sound like an expert, or at least understand a wine expert, use the following guidelines.

WINE *Descriptors*

Acidity is more of a factor in white wines than in red wines. Acidity gives white wines the majority of its taste. A wine with a high amount of acidity feels crisp. Usually, midpalate or the middle of the mouth is where the level of acidity is determined.

Body is the feel you get from the entire essence of the wine. It's not just taste, but weight in the mouth as well. Some wines seem heavier or bigger in the mouth and are considered full-bodied. Body is classified three ways: *full*, *light*, or *medium-bodied*.

Sweetness is noticeable as soon you put the wine in your mouth. When describing sweetness, or the lack of, use terms such as *dry*, which is the opposite of sweet, *off-dry*, or *sweet*.

Tannin is to red wines what acidic is to white wines. The amount of tannin makes wine bitter, firm (almost kind of chewy), or rich. Tannin is recognized and determined in the rear of the mouth. If the tannin level is high, your gums and the insides of your cheeks might feel dry after drinking. Red wine is described as *soft*, a gentle taste to the palate, *firm*, or *astringent*, which can make the mouth pucker a little.

Types of Wines

While new varieties of wines are constantly making their way into the marketplace, here is a list of the wines you are most likely to find on your favorite restaurant's wine list:

TYPES OF *White Wines*

Chardonnay, named after the grape that gives the wine its flavor, is one of the most popular white wines. Chardonnay is often identified by its oak flavor, but also infuses fruits such as apple and pineapple. Chardonnay wine has medium to high acidity and is full-bodied and usually dry. Less expensive Chardonnays are usually sweet.

Chenin Blanc wines range from bone dry to sugary sweet. This white wine has an earthy quality that is stronger that any of the other white wines. Chenin Blanc is one of the top three most acidic wines, next to Reisling and Sauvignon Blanc, and is also one of the best wines to store in the cellar because some of them can age up to ten years. The most popular and tasty Chenins are Vouvray and Savennièrs. The wine pairs well with all seafood.

TYPES OF *White Wines*

Pinot Gris/Pinot Grigio, which has several identities depending on where the grape is grown, is made from the black Pinot Noir grape. Although the color of the grape is dark and the wine is slightly darker than other whites, it is still considered to be a white wine. The color is not so dark that you can confuse it for a red wine. The flavor is medium to full-bodied, low acidity, with no oak taste and often has a hint of peaches or oranges. Pinot Grigio pairs well with pasta and fish and dishes that can be paired with a light, dry wine.

Reisling is at the opposite end of the taste spectrum from Chardonnay. Reisling rarely has an oak flavor and is a light-bodied wine. Most Reisling wines are sweet, but there are some that are not as sweet. The flavors tend to rage from fruity to flowery. Reisling is usually high in acidity, with low to medium alcohol levels. The range of tastes make Reisling one of the best wines to partner with all types of food. The Reisling grape hails from Middle Europe, with German Reisling being one of the most popular.

Sauvignon Blanc is often described as grassy or herb-like. The wine is medium-bodied and usually dry. It is often recommended that you drink Sauvignon Blanc "young and green." This rule-of-thumb means that Sauvignon Blanc wines are not usually stored in the cellar but best enjoyed right away (drinking it young) and best paired with leafy, green vegetables (drinking it green).

TYPES OF *Red Wines*

Cabernet Sauvignon is a full-boded wine with an impressive dark color. This particular wine has a deeper color and fruity aroma. The Cabernet Sauvignon grape makes wines that are high in tannin, so it is usually paired with other red grapes, like Merlot. Cab, as it is often called, is described as having flavors similar to cedar and the bell pepper.

Merlot has a deep color and is high in alcohol, with a chocolate or plum-like flavor. Merlot is a favorite wine among those who like to slowly sip a nice glass. When it comes to pairing with foods, it is not the first choice on the red wine list because of the heavy oak taste and low acidity.

Nebbiolo is known for its complex aromas and flavors that can range from roses, licorice, chocolate, and even leather. Because this wine is high in alcohol and acidity, the tannins are high in a young wine. Some versions of the wine are meant to be drunk young, but Barolo and Barbaresco, named for the Italian towns where the grapes are grown, are wines that should be stored a minimum of eight years before drinking. The color is very deep but over the years it can develop an orange tinge.

TYPES OF *Red Wines*

Pinot Noir is produced in limited quantities because the grape is very particular about the climate and soil where it is grown. Because the grape is so sensitive, vineyards call it the "heartbreak grape" and it is rarely blended with other grapes. Pinot Noir is lighter in color than both Merlot and Cabernet. With a fruity flavor, it has a high alcohol content, medium to high acidity and tannin. The high acidity makes it very versatile and easy to pair with all kinds of meals. Also, because Pinot Noir is so finicky, it is usually an expensive wine.

Syrah/Shiraz can range in taste from pepper to blackberries or even tar, depending on the origin of the grape. Quickly gaining in popularity because of its affordability, Syrah/Shiraz are full-bodied, deeply colored red wines. Because of its bold flavor, it is not usually blended with other grapes.

Zinfandel is very popular as a white Zinfandel, but both versions are actually made with a red grape. The flavors of red Zinfandel are rich with a raspberry or spicy aroma. The wine is high in alcohol with a medium to high tannin. Because the Zinfandel grape ripens later in the year, both red and white Zinfandel are sweet wines. The Zinfandel grape is one of the oldest grapes in California.

Fortified Wines

Fortified wines are wines that have alcohol added. When fortified with alcohol during fermentation, the wines are sweet. Port is made by adding alcohol *during* fermentation. The wines are dry when fortified *after* fermentations. Sherry wines use this process.

TYPES OF *Fortified Wines*

Port is considered to be the world's greatest fortified red wine. Port is mostly sweet and the wine is mostly red, although several styles exist, including White, Ruby, Tawny, Colheita, and Vintage Port. Vintage Port is the pinnacle of the wine. It is bottled at two years of age and is not considered mature until about twenty years. The wine often is enjoyed after dinner with a cheese platter featuring cheeses such as Cheddar, Gouda, and Roquefort. It is served at room temperature.

Sherry consists of two types: *fino,* which is light and very dry; and *oloroso,* which is rich and full, but also dry. Among dry Sherries, the most popular wines are Fino, Manzanilla, Manzanilla Pasada, Amontillado, Oloroso and Palo Cortado. Light, dry Sherries should always be served fresh. When ordering in a restaurant, ask how long the bottle has been open. Never accept a glass unless the bottle has been refrigerated or one where the bottle has been open more than two days. Dry Sherries are served with seafood, olives, hard cheeses, and nuts. Sweet Sherries are classified as Medium Sherry, Pale Cream, Cream Sherry, Brown Sherry, East India Sherry, Pedro Ximénez, and Moscatel. All of the sweet Sherries can be served with desserts or enjoyed on their own.

Wine and Entertaining

Depending on the gathering, wine can play a huge role in your party. It can influence the food you serve as well as the atmosphere of your party. The following information will ensure that you'll serve wine appropriately and expertly at every occasion.

Perfect Glasses for Wine

The best wineglasses for tasting and enjoying wine are clear, crystal wineglasses. Avoid colored glasses because they can prevent you from enjoying the wine's actual color as well as the clarity of the wine. Look for wineglasses that are round with a rim that lightly curves. This shape is best because it allows you to swirl the wine and release its fragrance.

Usually, white wine is served in a smaller glass than those used for red. Smaller glasses allow white wine to stay cold longer, while the larger glass used for red wine gives the reds more room to breathe. Hold red wine glasses around the globe while enjoying, and hold white wines by the stem to preserve the chill.

A good rule of thumb for pairing stemware with wine is the following: Red wine stemware should hold at least twelve ounces of wine. White wine glasses should only be ten to twelve ounces. For sparkling wines, a glass that holds eight to twelve ounces will work fine.

To add a nice touch to your party, provide each guest with a separate glass for each wine. This way, guests can sample different wines and compare them before deciding upon which they like. Most importantly, don't feel rushed (or rush your guests) to finish a glass before serving another type of wine.

Serving and Drinking

When buying wine for a party, the standard estimate of half a bottle per guest is a good place to start. Plan for more wine if you are having a dinner party with several courses or a cocktail party that will last longer than three hours.

Before serving, chill white wines for at least thirty minutes to an hour, to a temperature of 45–50 degrees. If white wine is too cold, the taste will be dull. Conversely, serving wine at a temperature warmer than 45 degrees emphasizes the alcohol taste and also mutes the flavor. Red wines should be served at room temperature, ideally, at a temperature of 50–65 degrees. Lighter reds should be served at the lower end of that range and full-bodied red wines at the higher end.

Always fill glasses with white wine a little less than half full to give the wine room enough to breathe, and makes swirling the wine in the glass less likely to spill. For red wine, fill a third of the glass

If you're planning a dinner party, you might want to serve more than one wine over the course of the meal. Most people usually serve a white with the first course and a red with the second course. However, if you decide that you want to serve more than the basic two wines, a good guideline to follow is: Serve white wine before red wine; serve light wine

cal says ...

When sipping wine, let a little bit of air into your mouth to allow the flavors of the wine to fully develop on your palate.

before heavy wine; dry wine before a sweet wine; and a simple wine before a rich, deep-flavored wine. Of course, this is just a guideline, not a rule. If you have a few wines that you are simply crazy about, or if your meal calls for a red wine, feel free to serve the wines you love or two reds. It's your party, so pour accordingly.

Ordering Wine in a Restaurant

When you are seated at your table, often your server will provide a wine list. Wine lists vary according to the restaurant's selection and are divided into categories such as white wines, red wines, Champagne and sparkling wines, and dessert wines.

Sometimes the list will rank the wines from dry to sweet and also list the origin of the wine and suggestions for food pairings. The price of the wine is always listed.

Ordering Wine with the Help of a Sommelier

After perusing the wine list, if you decide that you need assistance, ask to speak with the sommelier (a wine specialist) to help you make your wine selection. If the restaurant doesn't have one, ask to speak with the wine specialist, who will be someone on staff familiar with the wines, often the bartender.

When the sommelier arrives, you can point out two to three wines and ask which one the sommelier recommends. In addition to garnering useful information, you also are discreetly advising the sommelier of your budget. If he recommends another wine, the price should be close to the wines you inquired about. If you are not familiar with any of the wines, you also can mention the meal that you plan to order and ask for wine suggestions that would best complement the meal. Place your wine order before you order your food or along with your food to be sure it arrives in a timely fashion.

Wine Arrival

After the sommelier, or wine specialist, takes your order, the wine will be presented at your table. First, the sommelier presents the bottle with the label facing you so that you can inspect the bottle and verify that this bottle is what you ordered. You can feel the bottle to check for temperature if you like, but it's not necessary. If the bottle is correct, advise the server that you are satisfied with the inspection.

Next, the sommelier will remove the cork and place it in front of you. You then visually inspect the cork and smell it to determine if it is in good condition. If the cork smells funny, musty, or old, you should wait to see and smell the wine before deciding to reject the bottle.

If you've ordered a wine that needs decanting, the server will then decant the wine. Decanting is when the wine is transferred from the bottle to another container, to aerate the wine (allow it to breathe) or separate red wine from its sediment.

The most important rule of wine is to simply enjoy yourself and drink what you like.

The sommelier will then pour a small amount of wine into your glass and wait for your approval before filling your glass as well as your guests' glasses. You should then take a small sniff and then a little sip. If the wine tastes good, you should indicate to the server that the wine is fine by saying so or nodding your head.

This is the last chance for you to decide that you don't find the bottle of wine acceptable. If the bottle seems to be spoiled, ask someone else at your table for their opinion. What happens after you deem a bottle of wine as unsatisfactory depends on whether or not the sommelier agrees with you. If he concurs, he may bring you the wine list and ask you to make a new selection or bring you another bottle of the same wine. If he doesn't agree and believes that you don't understand the characteristics of the wine, he might then try to explain the origins of the wine and the flavors. If the reason you don't like the wine is simply the taste, then the lesson is at your expense.

If you accept the wine, the server will pour the wine into the other guests' glasses and then fill your glass. Also, once you've placed your order, keep in mind that an attentive waiter will make sure to refill your wine glass when it is close to empty. If you do not want a refill, you should leave enough wine in your glass so that the waiter can see it.

However, the most important rule of wine is to simply enjoy yourself and drink what you like. Sure, experiment with different types of wines to determine what suits your tastes. And if you like a red wine with your seafood, relax. The rules are really guidelines. Ultimately, what you enjoy and drink is entirely up to you.

CHAPTER 3

tips on tipping

On Friday night, ready for a night of bar hopping, Cal, Anissa, and I head to Beluga's, a classy lounge and one of our favorite spots. As usual, on a Friday night, happy hour is indeed happy. After working our way to the bar and ordering drinks, we spot an empty table and pounce on it. Settling into our seats, I look up to see a fine specimen of man appear next to us.

"Excuse me, can I buy you a round of drinks?" says the tall drink of water, smiling. We've barely sipped our first drinks, but we're no fools. Anissa quickly pipes up. "I'll have another watermelon martini. Thank you." He takes the rest of our orders and walks over to the bar. As soon as he is out of hearing distance, I look at my friends and sigh. "He is *gorgeous.*" Before they even had a chance to agree, Benjamin, as he introduced himself, came back to our table accompanied by two other guys, each of them holding a drink.

Making room at the table, we make polite introductions. The other two guys are equally handsome but quickly become *extremely* drunk. Cal and Anissa, not entertained by their antics, flash me the signal for "let's get out of here—now." Annoyed that I didn't have a chance to talk more with Benjamin, I let him know we're leaving. "Thanks for the drinks, Benjamin. It was great meeting you and your friends. Are you sure we can't chip in for the tab?"

"Of course not," he replies, signing his credit card slip and handing it to the waitress. "It was good meeting you too. Hopefully, I'll see you here again soon." Benjamin smiles at me and before I have a chance to change my mind, he and his friends disappear into the crowd.

As we're gathering our purses, ready to head to the next bar, the waitress returns to our table holding the credit card slip. "Can I ask you ladies if there was a problem with the service tonight?"

The three of us eye each other and Anissa quickly grabs the slip from her hand. Looking at the slip, she turns to us, looking perturbed. "Do you guys mind chipping in for a tip? That guy, whatever his name was, only tipped 10 percent of the bill. We've been drinking for more than an hour." She turns to the waitress to apologize. "You have been fighting the crowd to serve us and provided good service . . . I apologize. That is totally unacceptable!"

Wanting to redeem ourselves, Cal quickly hands the waitress $10 and I give her another $5. Anissa hands the bill—now with the proper tip—back to the waitress, who is patiently waiting for us to get her money together. "You sure are some classy women," she says gratefully. "Thanks so much."

"He seemed like a good guy," fumes Anissa as we head to the door. "I can't stand it when someone doesn't tip at least 20 percent." As we leave, I see Benjamin standing at the bar. When he smiles at me, I deliver a curt wave and walk out. So much for that. ❧

Tipping is an art form that should be mastered by all ladies. Learning how to tip gracefully is an important skill. Essentially, a tip is money that is earned by a person or people performing a service for you. The word "tip" originated in England and is an acronym for the phrase "to insure promptness."

Tipping can lead to tricky social situations. While you are expected to tip some people in certain professions, you should never feel obligated to tip if it's not deserved. Whenever you're in doubt about whether a tip is appropriate, veer on the side of caution and give a few dollars to the person performing the service. Read on to learn the details about when to tip, who to tip, and how much is appropriate.

Dining Out

Depending on the type of restaurant you are visiting, the number of employees that you are expected to tip can range from one person to several. Unless you are eating in a fast food or take-out restaurant, you can almost guarantee that you will at least require the service of a waiter.

At a restaurant, the amount to tip your server is 15 to 20 percent. You can tip less for subpar service, but for exceptional service, feel free to tip more than the guidelines suggest. If gratuity is automatically included in your bill, you may choose to tip above the standard amount for service that goes above and beyond. If you are dining at a buffet, tip the person who services your table 10 percent of the bill.

If a sommelier helps you to select your wine, tip him or her 15 percent of the cost of the wine. The sommelier's tip is in addition to the cost of the meal, which goes to your server. You can discreetly hand the sommelier a cash tip or include it in the amount on the bill as the entire tip. You also can designate that the tip is for the wine steward by noting that information on your bill.

Tipping the Maitre d'

Maître d'hôtel is French for "headwaiter." In the restaurant world, the maitre d' is the top staff person. It's great to have the maitre d' remember you and your favorite table, because this is the person who will seat you.

A maitre d' usually receives no tip, except a smile, unless he or she performs an extra service such as giving you a coveted table location. If the maitre d' performs an extra service, tip between $5 and $10. If you patronize the restaurant on a regular basis, tip the maitre d' every few visits. When tipping the maitre d', make the exchange smooth and seamless. Pass the money in a discreet handshake or small, brief encounter. It is considered rude to verbally offer the maitre d' money for service, as is often depicted in the movies.

Bar Tips

Just like waiters and waitresses, bartenders rely on tips to supplement their incomes. For a bar tab, tip about 15 percent of the total. However, if you only buy one drink, tip a dollar. Keep small bills handy for the purpose of tipping.

Hotel Tips

To assure better service when first checking into a hotel, give a big tip to the bellhop. Each time the bellhop performs a service for you and brings a requested item to your room tip $2. If the bellhop has to go the extra mile for something, then you should tip $5. As with restaurants, there can be several people you should tip when staying at a hotel. Here are some general guidelines about who to tip, and how much.

Hotel TIPPING

Chambermaid: Tip daily. The same maid may not service your room every night of your stay. If you wait until checkout time to tip for the entire stay, your tip may not go to the right person. Leave a tip in bills (not with spare change), mark your tip clearly, and leave it in an obvious place. Leaving cash or change in the room is not a clear enough signal, as a hotel maid must be very careful about taking anything from your room. Enclose the tip in a sealed envelope (check the desk drawer for hotel stationery) and mark it "Chambermaid." If you can't find an envelope, or the hotel doesn't provide one, wrap the bills in a blank sheet of paper, labeled appropriately. When you travel internationally, find out how to write "maid" or "Chambermaid" in the local language. Tip according to service and hotel type. In a luxury hotel, tip about $3–$5 each night. For an average hotel, $1–$2 per night is fine. If the maid goes above and beyond in service, such as providing extra soaps and shampoos, feel free to leave a dollar or two more.

Hotel TIPPING

Doorman: Tip $1 if he gets a taxi; $2 in bad weather.

Porter: $1 minimum per bag when checking in or out; more if bags are heavy.

Concierge: $10–$20 depending on the type of service. Theater tickets and last-minute arrangements all are special services and deserve a larger tip.

Hotel Door Persons: $2 for summoning a taxi by phone; $1 for hailing from street; $2–$5 if they opened the door for you each time you entered and left the hotel.

Beauty Salon

There's an age-old saying—beauty has a price. Indeed, maintaining healthy tresses, soft hands, and just looking good can cost money. In the salon, just as in a restaurant, tips are a part of the service. A basic list of those in the beauty industry follows on the next page.

If you have a relationship with your barber or hairdresser, by all means tip more. Minimally, tip whenever you visit. Tip more for or extra service like squeezing you in at the last minute or when you are exceptionally pleased with the results of your appointment.

Beauty Salon TIPPING

Hairdresser: 20 percent of your total bill if you are having an extra service like a cut, color, permanent. 15 percent for the basic wash and blow dry.

Shampoo assistant: $2

Manicurist or pedicurist: 15 percent of the total cost; including extra services such as acrylic, gel, or air brush designs (minimum $1.50).

Barber: 15 percent

A Dollar Here, A Dollar There— More Tipping Guidelines

Good service can be hard to come by but when you do find it, tipping to show that you appreciate the extra effort is a generous gesture. After all, the people and professions that we tip are providing a service and doing a good job. Not to mention that your tip is part of their pay. Be generous when it's deserved.

Tip Chart FOR SERVICES RENDERED

SERVICE PROVIDER	TIP AMOUNT
Chauffeurs	10–15 percent of fare
Cloakroom attendants	$1 for every coat. An additional 50 cents if you double coats on one hanger.

Tip Chart FOR SERVICES RENDERED

SERVICE PROVIDER	TIP AMOUNT
Restroom attendants	25–50 cents for providing a hand towel. Tip another dollar for additional service such as using perfume or hairspray.
Car washer	$2–$5, depending on level of service
Furniture deliverers/movers	$10–$20 per person
Dog groomer	$2–$5
Barista	$1
Masseuse	10–15 percent of bill minus sales tax
Personal trainer	15 percent of the cost of a session
Pizza deliverer	10 percent of bill excluding sales tax, $2 minimum
Shoe shiner	$2–$3
Sky caps (planes); Red caps (trains)	$1–$2 per bag
Taxi/limousine driver	15 percent
ANNUAL TIPS	**AMOUNT (enclosed in a holiday card)**
Babysitter	$25–$50 extra or a gift
Nanny	One week's pay and a week off
Doorman	$25–$50
Building superintendent	$50–$100
Gardener/landscaper	One week's pay
Housecleaner	One week's pay if an employee for less than a year; two weeks' pay if employed two years or more
Kennel manager	Food item that can be shared
Mail carrier	Food item that can be shared
Newspaper delivery person	$15–$25
Water delivery person	$15–$25

tips on tipping

47

Just as there are professions where tipping is required, there are also people that you do not need to tip. For example:

- ∞ Professionals, such as health care workers, attorneys, teachers, accountants, realtors, travel agents, and decorators
- ∞ Owners and mangers of businesses
- ∞ Ships' officers
- ∞ Train conductors
- ∞ Airline stewards
- ∞ Ushers at theaters, opera houses, and so on
- ∞ Plumbers, electricians, and other service employees, unless they come outside regular business hours as a favor
- ∞ Busboys

The ins and outs of tipping don't end here. Read on for more tips about this sticky social art form.

Quick Tips ON TIPPING

Keep small bills handy: When out on the town, always keep several one-dollar bills handy in an accessible pocket for ease of tipping.

Don't Ask For Change: Don't ask for change from the person you are tipping. Try to get change from somewhere else and then return with your tip at some point in the future.

Quick Tips ON TIPPING

Know the Tipping Policy: Some higher-end hotels institute a "no tipping policy." However, if you sign up for excursions or tours outside of the hotel (even those that don't cost extra), more than likely the drivers and the tour guides will expect tips. To be sure of the policy, ask if tipping is accepted when you book.

Bed and Breakfast Tipping Etiquette: In general, business owners are not given tips. When you book your room, ask about their tipping policy.

Tipping Is Never Required: Do not feel obligated to give a tip if the service was subpar. Tipping hotel staff, drivers, and anybody else is at your discretion and is recognition and a reward for excellent service. Certainly consider giving a larger tip for those who go the extra mile to provide personalized or exemplary service.

Tipping Etiquette Varies Worldwide: Tipping amounts vary in different countries. In some European countries, hotel and restaurant gratuities are included in your bill. Always check a travel guide for the proper tipping etiquette of the country you plan to visit.

Good service can be hard to come
by but when you do find it, tipping
to show you appreciate the extra
effort is a generous gesture.

Sticky Tipping Situations

Now that you have a better idea of who, what, when, and why to tip, sometimes the intricacies of tipping have to be discussed with friends—especially when you're hanging out and running a single tab. We all have friends who are stingy tippers. These are the situations that make tipping etiquette sticky—not occasions when the bellhop drops off our bags, but when dealing with friends and their personal finances. So the question is: When the time comes to pay up, do you pay more and take up your friend's slack or do you call your friend on the carpet about his or her poor tipping skills?

A delicate way to handle a friend or acquaintance who is a poor tipper is to divide the bill, including the tip, and then ask everyone to pay their share. If you have a friend who doesn't want to tip, you can then chip in the extra share or allow the tip to be a little less than deserved. Another way to handle that is to always ask for a separate check when you're out with the miserly friend. After all, you really can't demand that anyone tip the appropriate amount.

Which brings up another situation—if the person who is short with the cash is your boss or superior at work, never take it upon yourself to add more to the tip. Rather, allow the most senior person to divide the

meagan says ...

There are two reasons to tip above the norm: If service is exceptional and if you plan to return to the hotel or restaurant in the future. Visiting the same location has its perks: Big tippers are not forgotten by the staff.

bill and then you pay your portion. If you are on a date, it might be difficult to tell if the tip amount is short since you probably won't see the bill. If you do see the bill and determine that the tip is lacking, then by all means, add to the tip amount. Again, it's next to impossible to ask someone to tip more than they want to or have. There is rarely anything wrong with adding to a tip to be sure the amount is appropriate for the service performed—except when dealing with a boss or superior.

introductions and mingling

After the disaster dinner with Extraordinaire Cosmetics, I make sure I have my game face on when heading to the Skyscraper Advertising Awards event. I already know that there is one person I really want to meet tonight: Grace Alexander, the Vice President of Brand Marketing for PN&G, the top multicultural advertising agency in the nation and a huge competitor of ours.

Scanning the crowd for Grace, I meet eyes with a friend I used to work with, Cimone.

"Hey girl! How have you been?" asks Cimone. We exchange pleasantries and I tell her that I came to the reception with a plan. I want to meet Grace.

"She's here," says Cimone. "I saw her earlier." She eyes the crowd and then discreetly points out Grace. "If you get to meet her, congratulate Grace on her promotion. She's added global procurement to her repertoire," says Cimone, speaking quietly. "The position was just announced last week. She'll be impressed that you know."

"Her company isn't hiring right now, but she's always willing to meet with you or have lunch if you want to discuss something," says Cimone with a huge smile. I smile back and realize that one of those successful people who Grace helped was staring right back at me.

I thank her and spotted Grace holding court in the middle of a small crowd. I keep my eye on Grace and continue to meet and greet various people as I edge my way closer.

"Hey! Where have you been hiding?" asks Heidi, after she taps me on the shoulder. In my quest to keep my eye on Grace, I almost walked past her. Heidi works at PN&G and even though she is a competitor, I enjoy hanging around at industry functions—and her boss is none other than Grace Alexander.

While we're talking and catching up, out of the corner of my eye I see Grace heading over to talk to Heidi. After Heidi says hello, she turns to me. "Grace, I'd like you to meet . . ." Heidi trails off as I realize that she has forgotten my name.

Quickly, I jump in with, "Hi, my name is Meagan and I work with Xenith Advertising. Congratulations on your recent promotion."

"Thank you very much," says Grace, before peppering me with questions about myself, my job, and my aspirations. My confidence boosted by the interest she's showing in me, I ask her if it's possible to meet for lunch one day (soon).

"Sure," Grace replies, handing me her card. "Give me a call next week. I return all calls," she says. Wow! This is one classy lady. Grace leaves us after a colleague walks up and asks her if he can steal her away. I admit, he was smooth with it. I was kind of glad that he appeared when he did. I was running out of things to say.

"I'll see you two later," said Grace. "Make sure you give me a call."

"I certainly will. It was a pleasure meeting you." ❧

Meeting and greeting can be scary for most of us. The embarrassment of forgetting names or mispronouncing a name can be intimidating at best. However, making flawless introductions is easy with practice. The more you do it, the better you get at saying, "Lauren, this is Dr. Andrew Hunter. Andrew, this is Lauren, my next-door neighbor." See, it's really simple once you know the rules. The rules, you ask? Yes. Like everything proper, there are guidelines.

The Basic Rules of Introductions

When introducing yourself, use both your first and last name. If you're attending a social gathering and no one introduces you, simply jump right in when there is an opening and introduce yourself. If possible, add a bit of personal information about yourself. For instance, if you attend a networking function, you say, "Hello, my name is Erica Meadows. I work in the Marketing department at Tower Engines."

Always remember to stand whenever you are introduced to someone. If you are seated at a table or in a confined space where standing is awkward, shake hands and mention that you regret that you can't stand for the handshake.

In a less formal situation, you should still introduce yourself to others. If someone that you know joins your circle, you also can act as a host among the circle of friends and facilitate introductions.

Often, when introductions are made, a third-party will do the honors. The rule of adding a tidbit of information also applies when introducing others.

If you are introducing a married couple, you can introduce them as a pair. In all other situations, always use the full name of the person.

When determining who is introduced first, remember that younger people are introduced to older people and men are introduced to women. There is an exception to this rule—when the woman is the highest-ranking person, she is introduced to everyone else. Also, when introducing a client, the client is introduced first, regardless of the hierarchy or rank.

When there are dignitaries, clergy men or women, or any other VIP, introduce others to them as a sign of respect and always use his or her title. Remember that once a judge, ambassador, governor, or senator, the person remains so for the rest of his or her life. When introducing two VIPs to one another and they are of equal rank, introduce the one you know less well to the one you know better.

In a large group of people, introduce one person to a few people at a time. At a meeting, it's more efficient to go around the room and have everyone introduce themselves.

INTRODUCTION EXAMPLES

*"Mom, allow me to introduce Blake Robinson, Lisa's oldest son.
Blake, this is my mother, Mrs. Johnson."*

*"Kenya Thompson, I'd like to introduce you to Fred Heinz.
Fred, this is Kenya, a colleague of mine at Pressley River Communications."*

*"Mr. Mayor, I'd like to introduce Patrick Eisenstein.
Patrick, this is Mayor Jeffery Woodhouse."*

If Maria Gutierrez is a Vice President at your client's company and she is meeting Tom Ridenour, an Executive Vice President, the introduction would go like this:

"Maria Gutierrez, I'd like you to meet the Executive Vice President of Icon Products, Tom Ridenour."

Avoiding Introduction Blunders

The three biggest fears about the art of introductions are:

- ❧ Forgetting a name
- ❧ Mispronouncing a name
- ❧ Hearing the name, and, upon repeating it, slaughtering it

Don't fret. Those mishaps can happen to the smoothest of us. If you forget a name, either while making the introduction or after the introduction is made, simply say, "Your name has slipped my mind." The person should jump right in and introduce himself. If you mispronounce someone's name, apologize, ask for the correct pronunciation, repeat the name, and continue the conversation. Last, if you don't understand someone's name, ask the person to repeat it.

If you are being introduced to someone you've met before—but that person doesn't remember you—allow yourself to be introduced again. Never walk up to anyone and ask if they remember you. Always introduce yourself first.

And of course, after any introduction, always say, "I am pleased to meet you."

After initial introductions, the question of what to call someone (first name, Mr. or Mrs plus last name, and so on) may arise. The practice of using first names in the workplace and in informal settings is fine. However, before using a person's first name, always make sure that the person invites you to do so. Always use someone's title and err on the side of caution rather than appear too presumptuous and offend the person.

If speaking with a woman, and you're not sure if she prefers Ms., Mrs., or Miss, simply ask. If a woman is a PhD, medical doctor, or a military officer, use the appropriate title.

meagan says ...

The practice of giving background information when making introductions is to help start a conversation. When you are introducing two people, stick around a little to help jump-start the conversation. Don't introduce and then disappear.

Shaking Hands

In addition to standing for an introduction, a handshake is the appropriate follow-up. Not shaking hands is a clear form of rejection and is insulting to the other person. You should always shake hands under the following circumstances:

- ✺ When meeting someone and upon saying goodbye
- ✺ When someone enters your home or office that you do not know
- ✺ When renewing an acquaintance
- ✺ When greeting a host and being introduced to people
- ✺ When ending a business transaction or leaving a social or business event
- ✺ When meeting someone you already know outside the office or your home

Sometimes your hands are otherwise occupied. What to do then?

If you're introduced to someone and your hands are full, nod your head as you respond to the introduction. Likewise, if you are introduced to someone whose hands are full, don't wait for them to rearrange their packages or try to help them. Simply nod your head in response to the introduction. At a cocktail party, hold your glass in your left hand when introductions are made, so that you can shake hands and also offer a dry hand, rather than a cold, wet hand.

When wearing gloves as a part of formal attire, always remove them to shake hands. The same rule applies when wearing gloves outdoors. Remove them unless the weather is very cold.

From time to time you will meet someone who doesn't extend his or her hand after an introduction. The reasons why could range from their having a cold, a cultural reason, or even a phobia about germs. Regardless of the reason, when that happens, simply pull your hand back as unobtrusively as possible and continue the conversation or move on.

If you have an aversion to shaking hands, don't make it known. If you have a cold, simply tell the person you are being introduced to, "I would love to shake hands but I have a cold right now and would hate to get you sick." If you have a germ phobia, shake hands when introduced to someone and then keep your hands away from your hands and mouth. As soon as you can make a polite exit, excuse yourself and wash your hands in the powder room. You could also carry a small bottle of antibacterial lotion or gel in your purse. Not shaking hands, especially in a business environment, is a fast way to ruin a relationship that you might need.

The bottom line when it comes to handshaking is this: Whenever you're in doubt about whether to shake hands, it's best to extend your hand for the handshake.

introductions and mingling

Body Contact

In a business setting, body contact other than a handshake is inappropriate. Even if you and a friend or business acquaintance greet each other with a hug and kiss, always use caution when extending more than a handshake to others who might not feel as comfortable.

This is not to say that there won't be any hugs and kisses between 9 and 5. People who are comfortable and very familiar with each other might greet each other with more than a handshake especially when business is mixed with social interaction. However, it is always best to offer a handshake rather than a hug or a kiss.

When hugs and kisses are traded in a business setting, they are usually limited to brief exchanges but tend to fall under the following categories:

Hugs and Kisses IN A BUSINESS SETTING

Air Kiss: This air kiss is often seen depicted on TV among the rich and famous. It's a quick pucker and both parties touch cheeks. This prevents lipstick smudging and is still a greeting past the typical handshake. Sometimes, the air kiss is kissed on both cheeks.

Hugs and Kisses IN A BUSINESS SETTING

Actual Kiss: A peck on the cheek is best left outside of the boardroom, but two people who know each other fairly well might kiss on the cheek as a way of greeting when outside of the office.

Arm Clutch: The clutch is usually done with two men and is an extra show of affection other than the handshake. The two people will usually shake hands and then with the other free arm, grab the upper shoulder or arm.

Semi-Hug: Two people who have a close personal relationship might engage in a brief, one-armed clutch around the shoulders.

Bear Hug: The bear hug is a genuine two-arm, full embrace. This hug should be reserved for old friends and very close business associates and should not be used in the office.

Mingling

The art of mingling, interacting, and making yourself known in a crowd is important, especially for those vying for face time with important executives or other VIPs. Making mingling look carefree demonstrates that you are approachable, friendly, engaged, and most of all, interested in what others have to say. Mingling is not an introduction of yourself and then dominating the conversation, but an introduction and also applying

Mingling is not dominating
the conversation, but an
introduction and an application
of the art of listening.

the art of listening. When you're attending a work function, make sure that you don't spend the entire night talking to the same people. Converse with people you know and those you don't to get the most out of the event. Most importantly, attend a work event with certain goals in mind. A few to consider include:

- ∞ Always make sure you have plenty of business cards and give them out when appropriate.
- ∞ Stay well informed about timely issues and current events so that you'll have a few things to talk about when initiating a conversation.
- ∞ Attend all business events with a specific goal: to meet a certain person, a set number of people, obtain job leads, or get noticed. If you can, try to learn the names of the other attendees and some background information about them, and make sure to mention that information when you meet.
- ∞ Hold your drink in your left hand so that your right hand remains free, and dry, to shake hands.
- ∞ Do not use an open bar as an excuse to overindulge. Always stay sober so that you don't do anything you might regret.

Make eye contact, give a firm grip, and by all means don't get so nervous you forget your own name. Networking can be stressful, but if you use the tips mentioned you should be an expert at meeting, greeting, and shaking hands in no time at all!

eating tricky foods

With our busy schedules, Cal, Anissa, and I hadn't seen each other in a while, so we decided to get together for brunch at The Breakfast Grille. After handing over my car to the valet, I step inside. Inside, it's like a club—standing room only. After scanning the lobby filled with hip clientele, I realize I am the first to arrive. Feeling only slightly uncomfortable standing by myself, I order a mimosa while I wait for Cal and Anissa.

Thankfully, the ladies arrive just as I begin to sip my drink and Cal checks in with the hostess. Luckily, we have a reservation. Otherwise, we would be standing with the throng in the lobby.

As we are shown to our table, I notice several diners trying unsuccessfully to eat the eggs Florentine special I saw advertised on the menu board without looking like slobs. The combination of hollandaise sauce and oversized English muffin is not going well for most of the diners who are trying to enjoy their brunch without sacrificing their stylish outfits. Once we are seated, I open my menu to pick out something delicious for brunch—making sure to order something I can eat neatly. No need to look sloppy, especially in such a hip place. ❧

Eating foods that are messy, slippery, gooey, or filled with seeds can be tricky. Since some of the tastiest foods are also some of the messiest (such as corn on the cob), it is important to figure out a way to enjoy the food while still making sure it lands in your mouth and not in your lap. This chapter will give you an overview of some of the trickiest foods you'll encounter as a diner.

Starting Off Gracefully

When at a party or gathering, the host often serves appetizers before the meal. While it's lovely to mingle and munch on delicious canapés or enjoy hors d'oeuvres, soup, or salad at the table, if you're not careful, you can ruin your outfit (or your reputation as a lady) before you even begin the main course. Here's a rundown of how to handle the trickiest culprits when it comes to messy starters.

Caviar

If caviar is passed in a bowl or crock with its own spoon, serve a small spoonful onto your plate. Often, caviar is served with diced egg whites and yolks, minced onion, lemon slices, and toast points. If that is the case, use the individual serving spoons in each of the bowls to serve yourself small amounts of each accompaniment. Assemble a canapé with a knife, then use your fingers to lift it to your mouth.

If prepared caviar canapés are being passed at a cocktail party or reception, simply lift one off the plate and pop the entire thing into your mouth. Be sure to take the canapé that your fingers have touched.

Cheese

If served as an hors d'oeuvre, cheese is spread on a cracker with the knife that accompanies it.

When cheese is served with a salad, you can spread it on a cracker or bread with either a fork or knife. Soft cheeses, such as Brie or feta, are always spread with a salad or butter knife.

When enjoying dessert cheeses that are served with fruit, simply quarter, core, and/or pare the apples or ripe pears, and then eat the cheese with a fork and the fruit with either a fork or your fingers. Alternate between bites of fruit and cheese.

Shrimp Cocktail

If you are eating your own shrimp cocktail and it is served in a stemmed glass, pick the shrimp up with an oyster fork and bite off a mouthful at a time. If you are sharing cocktail sauce, spread some sauce on your plate and use that sauce to dip your shrimp before each bite. If shrimp are served on a dinner plate, they can be cut with a knife and fork.

Soups

Soup may be served either in a soup plate or in a cup, depending on the type of soup and the formality of the meal. All soups are eaten in the same manner: Hold the soup spoon or bouillon spoon as if holding a pencil. Spoon the soup away from you toward the center of the top of the bowl, and then sip the soup from the side—not the end/point—of the spoon.

When resting between bites, rest the spoon in the bowl. After finishing the course, rest the spoon on the saucer or plate beneath the cup or bowl. Do not leave the spoon in the cup or bowl.

Do not blow on soup to cool it down. If the soup is too hot, simply try to cool it by stirring it. Or, spoon soup from the edges of the bowl first—this area may be cooler.

Tiny crackers or croutons can be added to soup, a few at a time in whole pieces. Larger crackers should be eaten separately, except when eating thick and hearty soups such as chowders at informal meals, when you can add a few pieces of cracker at a time.

The number one rule when it comes to enjoy soups, stews, and chowders? Always drink them quietly.

anissa says ...

If coffee or tea spills on your saucer, it is acceptable to ask for a new saucer. If a new saucer is not available, or it is inconvenient to ask for one, use paper napkins in the saucer to absorb the spilled tea and let the napkin remain.

Salad

Salad is always eaten with a fork. Oversized pieces should be cut, however, to avoid having pieces fall off your fork. When a salad is served at the same time as your main course, do not transfer it to your dinner plate. If no salad plate is provided, put the salad on your butter plate. You can use a piece of bread or a roll against a fork to help push the salad onto it.

Coffee: When drinking coffee, tea, and other hot drinks, a saucer may be provided under the cup for your teaspoon. If there isn't a saucer, the spoon may be placed facedown on a place mat or on the edge of a butter plate or dinner plate. Do not drink from a coffee mug with a spoon in it.

Hot Tea: When tea is served in its own pot, the tea bag sits on the plate next to the pot. Place the tea bag into the pot—not the cup—to brew the tea. When the tea bag is served at the side of a cup of hot water, place the tea bag into the cup. After dunking a tea bag, squeeze the excess liquid by pressing the bag against the side of your cup with a spoon or place the tea bag in your spoon and wrap the string around the spoon and bag. The tea bag should then be placed on the edge of the saucer after squeezing the excess liquid. If there is not a saucer, request one so that you have a place to rest the bag. Do not drink tea with a spoon in it.

Iced Tea: If your iced tea has a lemon wedge perched on the rim of the glass, squeeze it into your glass, making sure you cup it with your hand to keep it from squirting. If it's a slice, simply drop it in the tea.

Cocoa: Never blow on a hot drink to cool it. Stir it quietly and/or wait until it cools. Never dunk anything into your drink, even it's cocoa or coffee—not even a donut.

Brandy: A brandy snifter should be warmed to bring out the bouquet. This is done by rolling the bowl of the glass between both of your hands, and then cupping the snifter in your hand.

The Main Course

The risk of appearing messy doesn't end with the appetizer course. Avoid appearing sloppy by following these guidelines while enjoying your entrée.

Pasta

There are many types of pasta commonly served, and just as many ways to enjoy it. Spaghetti is eaten with a fork. To eat spaghetti neatly, use your fork to pick up a few strands and twirl them until they are wrapped around the fork. If you need the aid of a large spoon to help wind the spaghetti, that is fine. However, you should never lift the spoon from the plate. You can also use a small piece of bread to buttress the fork if you want to avoid the often frowned-upon spoon. Never cut spaghetti.

Thicker noodles such as macaroni, lasagna, or cannelloni can be cut with a fork. If pasta is served with sauce and grated cheese on top of the pasta, you can toss it with a spoon and fork prior to eating. If sauce remains after finishing the noodles, you can sop it up with fork-speared bread.

Pizza

Most of the time, you should enjoy pizza as finger food. However, this is not always ideal. If the consistency is soft and it would be difficult to hold the pizza, you can use a knife and fork. An especially large slice of pizza or a pizza that has many toppings on it, again, making it soft, can be eaten with a knife and fork. A pie-shaped slice of pizza should be held in your hand with the sides curled up to avoid losing the filling.

Vegetables

While it's important to get your greens, they can be tricky to eat gracefully. This next section will help you handle the more vexing vegetables while remaining neat and poised.

Artichokes

This funny-looking vegetable is served stuffed or plain and usually with hot drawn lemon butter, hollandaise sauce, mayonnaise, or vinaigrette. To enjoy it, tear a leaf from the artichoke. Hold the pointed tip and place the wider end in your mouth. Pull the artichoke leaf through your teeth to remove the inside, which is edible. If the artichoke is served with a thin sauce, such as vinaigrette, dip the wide end and quickly bring it to your mouth. If served with a thicker sauce, use the edible end (the wider part, not the pointed tip) to dip into the sauce.

Discard the thin, inner leaves when you reach them. It is proper to steady the artichoke by holding it on the bottom with a fork and using your fingers to pull off the leaves. Do not eat the hairy center. Simply remove it and eat the vegetable's "heart."

Asparagus

Depending on how it is prepared, asparagus can be eaten as a finger food. Firm asparagus may be picked up with your fingers and the tips dipped into any sauce that may be served and eaten from the tips down. Limp asparagus should always be eaten with a fork or knife and fork. However, at a formal dinner, it is best to use a fork and knife.

The important thing is to
maintain your confidence and to
never allow the etiquette involved
to diminish your experience.

Cherry Tomatoes

Eat cherry tomatoes with your fingers except when they're served in a salad. For ease of dining, select small tomatoes that will fit in your mouth. To prevent squirting, don't eat them bite by bite.

If the cherry tomatoes are large, pierce the skin gently with your front teeth, bite off half and then finish eating the rest of the tomato.

Corn on the Cob

Fresh corn on the cob is typically served at informal gatherings and can be broken in half to make it easier to handle. The trick to staying neat is not to butter or season the entire piece of corn at once and to focus on eating only a few rows or a section at a time. The best way is to butter, salt, eat, and then repeat until the corn is gone. This method helps to keep messiness on your hands and face to a minimum. Eating across the cob or around the cob is a matter of choice—both get the job done.

Potatoes/French Fries

Potato chips and shoestring potatoes are finger foods. Small French fries also can be enjoyed as a finger food, but the use of a fork is preferable. If fries are large or too big to manage as a finger food, cut them with your fork. Never dangle a fry on your fork and nibble away at it. If using ketchup or any other condiment, spread some on your plate, and either use your fingers or a fork to dip the fries.

Baked potatoes are usually served with a cut down the middle, If not, cut the top with a knife, open the potato wider with your fingers or a fork, and then add your desired condiments and seasonings. You can eat the skin of the potato as you eat the potato filling. Do not pick up the skin after eating the inside of the potato and eat it. Enjoy the skin along with the rest of the potato.

I've Got a Bone to Pick With You . . .

As you well know, some entrées are served with the bones still in them. This can be an exceptionally awkward dining situation, but don't let that stop you from enjoying your meal. One rule that applies to all meats is that bones should be placed to one side of the dinner plate.

One meat that is sometimes served "bone-in" is chicken. If the occasion is informal, like a barbeque or a picnic, you may eat chicken with your hands—but try to use one hand only. If the situation is formal, cut the meat from the bones with your knife and fork. If you are unsure of whether to use your hands or utensils, you can do two things: Wait to see what the hostess does, or use the knife and fork and leave whatever cannot be picked up with your utensils on your plate.

When dining at a fine restaurant, the kitchen chef will often debone or cut duck, quail, or hen into manageable pieces. If doing the work on your own, cut the wings and legs off the bird and then eat the body with a knife and fork.

It is appropriate to ask the waiter for help in cutting up the bird or to request a sharp knife, if one was not provided.

Although you can eat the wings and legs of the bird using your fingers, never pick up the body of the bird.

Cut veal, pork, or lamb chops with a fork and sharp knife in the center, or "eye," of the meat. In formal or restaurant situations, never pick up a bone and eat off it. In an informal setting, chew away but only if the bones are free of gravy.

When you order fish in a restaurant the kitchen chef may debone the fish before serving. However, if the fish is served with bones, remove small bones with your fork or your forefinger and thumb, while being discreet. Never spit the bones (or anything else) into your napkin.

Fruits

Juiciness is what makes eating fruit so enjoyable—but it's also what makes it difficult to do so neatly. How you should eat fruit varies from type to type, as explained here:

HOW TO *Eat Fruit*

Apples and Pears: An apple or pear should be picked up with your hand and placed on your plate. It is acceptable to peel the fruit in a spiral fashion before eating. If peeling the fruit is too cumbersome, place the fruit on a dessert plate, then cut it in half, core, and cut it into small pieces. The fruit is then eaten with a fork and a fruit knife. Pick up the smaller pieces of fruit with your fingers if the meal is informal.

HOW TO *Eat Fruit*

Bananas: In all informal situations peel and eat a banana without silverware. If a banana is served at a more formal situation, peel and cut it with a knife (preferably a fruit knife), and eat the banana with a fork.

Berries, Cherries, and Grapes: Berries are enjoyed with a spoon, with or without cream. Cherries and grapes are eaten with the fingers. Dispose of pits and seeds discreetly into your hand and deposit them in a napkin if the situation is informal or on your dessert plate if at a table.

Grapefruits, Oranges, and Tangerines: When grapefruit is halved, eat it with a teaspoon or a pointed grapefruit spoon. Peel oranges with a sharp knife and eat in sections with a fork or with fingers. If an orange has been precut, eat it like a grapefruit—with a grapefruit spoon or teaspoon. Tangerines are peeled by hand and eaten piece by piece. If the white covering is especially thick, this can be peeled off as well.

Melon: Melon wedges—whether honeydew, cantaloupe, or any other melon—are eaten with a spoon or cut from the rind and into pieces with a knife and fork. Melon balls, with or without syrup, are eaten with a fork. When eating watermelon, use a fork to pick out as many seeds as you can before eating the meat of the melon with your fork.

Peaches and Plums: Peaches, plums, and nectarines should be cut in half and then quartered. Remove the stone with a knife. The skin can be peeled, but it is perfectly acceptable to cut the fruit into smaller pieces with the skin still intact and then eat the fruit with your fingers.

eating tricky foods

HOW TO *Eat Fruit*

Pineapple: Pineapple slices are always eaten with a knife and fork.

Strawberries: Large strawberries may be eaten whole as a finger food, holding them by the stem. Eat a strawberry in a few bites and then leave the stem on your plate. If strawberries are served in cream, use a spoon.

Hands-on Foods

Occasionally, you may find yourself enjoying finger foods while dining outside of your home, whether at a restaurant or party. Thankfully, it is possible to eat finger foods without making a mess. So bring on the bacon, the sandwiches, and the shellfish. One finger food that you may dine on at brunch is bacon. When bacon is cooked crisp, consider it a finger food. When it's soft, or if it has any fat, use your fork and knife.

The following foods are meant to be finger foods or eaten with the hands: corn on the cob (as covered in the vegetable section), ribs, clams and oysters on the half shell, lobsters, sandwiches, dry cakes, cookies, certain fruits (see individual listings), crisp bacon, chicken wings in informal situations, small French fries, radishes, olives, and celery.

When finger foods are offered on a platter, place them on your plate or napkin before you put them into your mouth. If in doubt on how to eat something, always follow the host or hostess.

Bread and Rolls

Restaurants often serve bread to start a meal. Whenever a bread basket is placed in front of you, it is your responsibility to pass the bread to the others who are dining. If the table is round, offer the bread to the person on your right and help yourself to the bread *after* it is passed around and returns to you. If the table is square, or rectangular, help yourself *first* and then pass to your right.

If the bread is served in a basket covered with a napkin, take a small portion of the napkin in your left hand and hold a section of the bread without touching more than the piece you will eat, and tear the bread with your right hand. Small biscuits do not have to be broken, nor do bread sticks. If the bread is served warm, always be sure to re-cover the bread to keep it warm.

Tear slices of bread, rolls, or muffins in half or in small pieces before buttering and eating. Bread sticks can be buttered on one side. Cut Danish pastries (sweet rolls) into halves or quarters and butter each piece as you eat it. Do not butter the entire slice of bread or roll at once.

If using butter from a serving dish, take it from the dish and place it on your bread-and-butter plate, not directly on the bread. Do not use the knife with the butter dish to butter your bread. If no knife rests on the butter dish, you may use your own knife. Butter the bread on the plate or just slightly above it.

Small sandwiches and canapés are eaten with your fingers. Large sandwiches should be cut before lifting and eating. A hot sandwich that is served with gravy requires a knife and fork.

Shellfish

Although many types of shellfish are eaten with a fork and knife, there is almost always some sort of handiwork involved. Shellfish is one of the messiest foods to enjoy as the food itself is often watery and is served with drawn butter. For clams and oysters served raw on the half shell, squeeze lemon juice (with one hand over the wedge or slice to prevent squirting) directly onto the clam or oyster—not into the sauce. Extract the clam or oyster with a small shellfish fork while holding the shell against the plate with your free hand. You may dip the meat into your own sauce container and then eat it. Or spread a dollop of horseradish and cocktail sauce onto the clam or oyster before eating it.

Fried clams, oysters, scallops, or shrimps should be cut with a fork and eaten. As for oyster crackers, it is permissible to drop them into the sauce and retrieve them with a fork.

Fantail shrimp can be lifted with your hands by the tail, dipped into a sauce, and then eaten. However, make sure you leave the tail. All empty shells should be piled on a second plate.

To eat crab, remove the legs with your fingers and gently remove the meat out of them. Break the back and open and remove the meat with a small fork. With soft-shell crabs, the entire crab—shell and all—is edible and should be eaten with a knife and a fork.

Lobster, although delicious, is very messy. For that reason, it is often enjoyed with a lobster bib. To eat a lobster, the first step is to twist off the claws. Crack each claw with a nutcracker and remove the meat with a fork. Then, remove the tail from the body. You can remove the meat by using your hands to straighten the tail and a fork to remove the meat. Twist off the lobster legs and remove the meat. Next, break the body in half lengthwise and use your fork to reach small pieces of meat. If you desire, you can eat the tomalley and the coral. The tomalley, which is the lobster's liver, is identified by its green color; the coral (or roe) is a mass of lobster eggs.

Spreads, Sauces, Sides, and Such

Depending on the type of food you are eating, you may be offered various sauces or spreads to accompany your meal. Enjoying them without spilling sauce on yourself or the tablecloth requires some delicate dining.

As discussed previously, always apply small pieces of butter to breads, rather than buttering the entire roll or piece of bread. This makes it much easier to eat neatly. Buttering vegetables is considered an insult to the cook and you should refrain from doing so.

Mustard, horseradish, jelly, apple butter, and cranberry sauce should be spooned onto your plate next to the meat or other food item they are meant to accompany. Using your fork, dip the meat into the sauce to enjoy.

Gravy or sauce should never be poured onto everything on your plate—regardless of how much you like it. Gravy should be used only for the dish intended and even then, sparingly. Soaking up the extra gravy with a fork-speared piece of bread is a wonderful compliment to the cook. Eat the remaining gravy with small pieces of bread at a time.

Liquid sauces, such as duck, soy, or cherry sauce, can be poured directly onto the meat. Always use a small amount, so that you don't mask the taste of the meat.

Jellies, jams, and preserves for rolls and biscuits should be spooned onto the side of your butter plate and spread on small pieces of bread with a knife. If a spoon isn't available for serving, wipe your knife on the edge of your plate before spooning the jelly from the serving bowl.

If honey is offered as a sauce, take a small amount of honey with a spoon and then drop it onto your butter plate.

Garnishes

Use a serving spoon (if one is provided) to place garnishes such as olives, celery, or radishes on your butter plate. If you do not have a butter plate, use your main dish. Never reach for garnishes and then put them directly into your mouth. If you want to salt them, shake some salt onto your plate, not the garnish, and use your fingers to dip and eat them. Eat olives whole and remove the pits by disposing of them into a tight fist and then place the pits on your butter plate.

Eat pickles with your fingers when accompanied by a sandwich. Use a knife and fork when pickles are served with meat.

Dill, parsley, and watercress are eaten with a fork when served as part of the meal. They may be eaten with fingers but not when they are covered with salad dressing or sauce.

Thin lemon slices are decoration; lemon wedges or halves are meant to be squeezed on your food or into your drink. To season your food, pierce the lemon wedge with a fork and squeeze it over the food, cupping your hand to shield any squirting. Some restaurants cover the lemon with cheesecloth to prevent spurts of juice.

Just Desserts

If you've saved room, there's no better way to end a meal than with a dessert. While you're almost to the end of dinner, it's not time to forget your manners. Here are some tips to keep in mind while enjoying dessert.

- ∾ When served as an accompaniment to cake or pie, eat ice cream with a dessert spoon or fork. When served alone in a dish, eat ice cream with a teaspoon or dessert spoon. Often, sorbet is used as a palate cleanser between courses. Then you only need to have a small taste; it's not necessary to finish the entire dish. When sorbet is served along with meat or with fruit, it is eaten with a fork. Use a spoon if sorbet is served as a dessert.
- ∾ Pie is eaten with a fork, unless it's served à la mode (with ice cream). Then both a fork and spoon should be used.

- A fruit tart usually is eaten with a fork. But if a tart is served with both a fork and a dessert spoon, use the fork to hold it on the plate, and cut and eat it with a spoon.
- If you are eating a creamy pastry, it's best to use a fork rather than holding it in your hand, in order to keep the filling from coming out the other end.

Although remaining ladylike while eating is not always an easy task, keep in mind the guidelines in this chapter, and you'll be on the road to dining divinely. The important thing is to maintain your confidence and to never allow the etiquette involved to diminish your dining experience.

CHAPTER 6

parties and
entertaining

In an attempt to get all of my busy friends and coworkers together for a night of socializing, I've taken it upon myself to throw a cocktail party in my home. After preparing canapés, stocking the bar, and cleaning my house from top to bottom, I am more than ready to cut loose when the first guest arrives.

A half hour into the party, everything is going fine. The music is upbeat and my guests seem to be enjoying themselves. In between sips of wine and cocktails, I flutter about the room checking on my guests. Confident that everyone is having a good time, I walk into the kitchen to check and see if the Brie is warmed up.

As I remove the warmed cheese from the oven, the doorbell rings and I walk into the living room to see Cal, not budging from her seat right next to the door. *What's wrong with her?* I fume silently as I open the door. Standing there is Rachel, a friend from work, and three other ladies whom I've never seen before. Trying to remain poised, I greet my guests as I let them in.

"Welcome to my humble abode," I say with a sweeping wave of my hand. "Let me take your coats and introduce you to everyone." Introducing Rachel to Anissa, Rachel then introduces her two friends and a five-year-old girl—all of whom were not invited. Trying not to appear taken aback at the uninvited guests, particularly the child, I maintain my composure and keep smiling.

As I make introductions, everyone politely says hello and Anissa helps me to gather up some extra empty chairs for the new guests. I pour drinks for the ladies and a glass of juice for the child.

After everyone is situated, I walk into the kitchen with Anissa closely behind me.

"Can you believe she brought friends *and* a kid?" I ask. "It's so inappropriate to bring a child to a cocktail party."

"Well maybe she couldn't find a babysitter," Anissa says.

"Maybe, but she wasn't even invited!"

By this time, everyone has a bit of food and a drink in hand so I figure I should try to relax, mingle, and enjoy myself. ❧

Planning the perfect party takes time, patience, and if you're lucky, a little panache. There are so many different things to worry about. If you're the type to write a checklist, you'll find that the list can grow longer and longer.

The décor, the guests, the food, music, tables, chairs, and so on—all of those items are important for a party. But the best ingredients for the perfect party are great guests and tasty food. If you have those two, you'll always have a throw-down gig.

Getting the Party Started

First things first: you need to determine what type of event you are planning. This decision might sound trivial, but, actually, it has major ramifications since all other ensuing decisions will be based on the type of party you decide to host. Will it be casual, formal, have a theme, include children, or even require guests to be in costume? Once that is set, your menu, your guests, décor, and everything else follows suit.

Types of Parties

The general rule of thumb is that most parties, regardless of the occasion, fall under three umbrellas: sit-down dinner party, buffet, or a cocktail party.

For each, the standard guidelines differ a bit, ranging from the type of food that will be served, to the décor, to the seating arrangements.

Sit-Down Dinner Party

This setting is right for a small amount of people—typically ten people maximum, or enough guests to fill one large table. A dinner party is a cozy affair and designed to spark plenty of lively conversation. The food served should include very light hors d'oeuvres (nuts or crackers), wine, nonalcoholic beverages, and the main course. Remember that the meal is the main event, which is why hors d'oeuvres should be very light.

The menu should include a variety of foods with different textures and colors. Foods also should coincide with the season and the weather.

For a dinner party, the host will have to inventory her place settings to be sure that she has enough silverware, plates, linen napkins, and glasses. For a sophisticated touch to the dining table, she can add an appropriate centerpiece.

Buffet

A buffet-style party gives the host plenty of options since the food is prepared well in advance. Another plus to a buffet party is that it can be held at any time of day, and the foods can be breakfast, lunch, or dinner foods. Even though a buffet is less formal than a dinner party, the host should still be sure that there is enough seating for everyone. The host will need an assortment of prepared food, a large table for the food, and another for the drinks (including wine, beer, nonalcoholic beverages), plates, silverware, and glassware. The most important rule is to serve food that will taste great at room temperature, or use chafing dishes to keep the food warm throughout the meal.

Since guests will serve themselves, you run the risk of running out of food. For better control, limit portion sizes by slicing the food in advance.

Remember, also, it's easier to stick to a theme so that all the foods mesh well together on the plate and the palate. Avoid foods that require a knife, although if a guest requests a knife, you should provide one. Do not put knives on the table; simply comply with requests.

Cocktail Party

The cocktail party differs from the other two types of parties as it does not center around food. Only hors d'oeuvres are served, which can be fancy or plain, but certainly plentiful since they will be the only food that is served.

A cocktail party should have a large enough crowd so that people feel comfortable whether they are sitting or standing. The components that make a great cocktail party—besides great guests—are a table for the bar, liquor, mixers, beer, wine, nonalcoholic drinks, ice, glasses, and bar tools.

Invitations

Nowadays, invitations to an informal event can be extended via phone, e-mail, or traditional snail mail. The method depends on how the guest

meagan says ...

When planning your hors d'oeuvres to be served at a cocktail party, keep in mind the appetizers should be small enough to fit on cocktail plates or napkins or eaten as a finger food. When preparing an appetizer menu, also remember to serve foods that are not accompanied by heavy sauces, which will help your guests keep their blouses and shirts clean.

wants to present the party and what expectations you want (or don't want) to set. Whatever medium you select, all the different types of invites have benefits associated with them. Mailed invitations are always correct and help set the ambiance of the party. They also serve as a tangible reminder of the event. For a formal event, a mailing, with a three- to six-week advance notice for guests, is still required.

Phone invitations, on the other hand, offer the advantage of an immediate RSVP. Sending invitations via e-mail is quick, and programs such as Evite.com keep track of your guest list and also allow guests to respond with a click of the button.

Regardless of the method you choose, all guests should be invited in the same manner so that no one feels slighted. All invitations should include the following information:

PARTS OF AN *Invitation*

Name of the host or hostess.

The type of party. The invitation should be as specific as possible so that guests know what to wear and whether the event is formal or informal.

Date and Time. The date and time is the most important information on the invitation. If the party is divided into a reception and a main event, the invitation should spell out that information as well. If you want the party to end at a certain time, you should include an end time on the invitation. If it's an event such as a housewarming and guests will be staggered, it's always wise to include the time the party will end.

PARTS OF AN *Invitation.*

Address and location of the party.

RSVP information. If you want guests to respond to the invitation, be sure to include RSVP information, phone number, an e-mail address, and a deadline for response.

Extra information. This is where the dress code would be clearly spelled out as well as whether gifts are expected or discouraged. Extra information also lets guests know if the party is a surprise so that invited guests won't ruin the event for the guest of honor.

Who is invited. The invitation, if mailed or sent via e-mail, should be addressed to everyone who is invited to the event. If you are inviting people over the phone, then you should say to the guest, "We hope you and William can join us at the party," which leaves out the names of their children. When guests call and RSVP, you can remind them that the event is for adults and ask, "Will you be able to find a babysitter for that night?"

On the other hand, if there are no restrictions on who is invited, make that clear on the invitation or when inviting guests over the phone. The invitation can say, "Please feel free to bring a friend or date," or you can tell your guest that "friends are welcome to join you in the festivities."

RSVPs

The rule of thumb is that if you ask guests to RSVP, you should plan to add 10 to 20 percent over that number since some guests will not RSVP. If you don't ask for a response, plan for 70 to 80 percent of the invited guests to attend the event. If you want an exact head count, you can contact guests that have not responded.

Party Timeline

Planning a successful party, regardless of the size, takes planning and preparation. You need to make a to-do list to keep track of all party items and also to be sure that you haven't forgotten any important elements.

A sample timeline for planning a party follows:

8 WEEKS OR MORE IN ADVANCE

- Set a date and time.
- Decide what kind of party to throw (for example, buffet, cocktail, sit-down dinner, themed).
- Determine the location. If you will not have the party at your house, reserve the location as soon as possible.
- Start your guest list.
- Establish a budget.
- Decide on a menu.

- Figure out if you will need to hire servers or caterers and book them.
- Choose what kind of entertainment you will have. If you decide to have a band or a DJ, reserve them.

6 TO 8 WEEKS IN ADVANCE

- Send out invitations.
- Take inventory of the menu and the number of guests and determine what extras you need to rent.
- Arrange for all rentals.

4 WEEKS IN ADVANCE

- Take inventory of beverages, mixers, and liquor, and restock.

TWO WEEKS IN ADVANCE

- Make sure you take note of the space where the party will be held so that you can remember to move any furniture before the party.
- Plan your decorating scheme and colors. If using a florist, consult with her as to the price and availability of the flowers that fit your theme.
- If using your own linens, check your tablecloths and cloth napkins for holes and stains. Wash and iron those that need it.
- Arrange a place away from the entry for guests to put their coats and umbrellas.

1 WEEK IN ADVANCE

∾ Contact all the caterers, musicians, rental company, and confirm arrival details and pick up.

∾ Call guests that you haven't heard from to confirm the number of guests.

∾ Give one final cleaning, especially the areas where the guests will be.

1 DAY IN ADVANCE

∾ Start decorating and setting tables.

∾ Receive all rentals and flowers.

∾ Check bar and cocktail supplies.

∾ Set up the bar area and put out glassware, liquor, mixers, bar tools, and bar goods that don't need to be chilled.

∾ Select party music.

∾ Place candles around the house.

DAY OF EVENT

∾ Complete decorations.

∾ Assemble your serving platters.

∾ Light candles or start fire in the fireplace, if the season permits.

∾ Turn on music.

∾ Get dressed, leaving plenty of time so that you are pleased with how you look.

anissa says ...

When guests arrive, it is the job of the hostess to greet, circulate, and make sure everyone is having a great time. Make sure that drinks stay refreshed, buffet dishes are refilled with food, and circulate among the guests to introduce them to others. Try to be sure that you spend a little time with each guest.

- ∾ Check on caterer.
- ∾ Set out appetizers.
- ∾ Greet guests when they arrive.
- ∾ Enjoy yourself.
- ∾ Serve food.
- ∾ End the party with desserts.
- ∾ Put your feet up after the guests leave!

Preparing the Menu

Planning a menu is never easier than when your party is themed. If you decide to have a Halloween party or Christmas party, then your menu would coincide with foods that are associated with the corresponding time of year.

Another idea to help plan the menu is to select foods that are in season around the date of the party. For instance, you could serve asparagus and salmon in the spring; cherries and lobster in the summer; steak and pumpkins in the fall; and for winter, turnips and beef. To determine what foods go together, keep in mind the following five characteristics:

1. **Color.** Make sure that foods are a variety of colors, rather than the same. For instance, a white soup as a first course can be followed up with a red, purple, or yellow second course.

2. **Size.** If you serve a small pasta dish as a first course, follow up with a large entrée of poultry or fish to contrast the size between the two courses.

3. **Taste.** For taste, try to offer contrast between courses. Go from a light dish to a heavier one, like a salad followed by a hearty stew. Or, you can always try raw, uncooked foods and then follow up with a cooked course.

4. **Texture.** If you serve a smooth, light soup for one course, the next can be a crispy or crunchy meat or vegetable.

5. **Temperature.** Go from a hot, steaming first course to a room temperature entrée or even a frozen dessert.

Deciding on the Number of Courses

For most people, two to three courses is plenty to prepare and eat. There is no correct number of courses to serve, however. Your decision could be based on your experience cooking, the occasion, the amount of help you have, and your own time and energy. If you are new to entertaining, then fewer courses would work best for you. If you have a certain budget that you want to adhere to, that's another reason for serving only a few courses.

Sometimes you do want to serve more courses. If you want to show off your culinary skills, lengthen the evening, or even spotlight a favorite food, then, by all means, extend the menu beyond two to three courses.

How Much Food Should You Prepare?

Running out of food is every hostess's nightmare. After deciding on a menu and confirming the number of guests to expect, you have to decide how much food you need to prepare. So, if you're not a professional chef, how do you calculate how many string beans, filets, and cream puffs to buy?

Also, you can consider the following rules: If you are having dinner later in the evening, after 7 P.M., consider smaller portions. If your guests are all coming to your house after another event, your portions can be a bit larger because your guests will have foregone food for a while. Also, if the menu you prepared is loaded with heavy foods, you can serve a little less since people will fill up quicker.

Hiring a Caterer

Having a caterer to help you prepare and serve food at your party is a great idea. Although the cost of the caterer is certainly more expensive than preparing the food and serving it yourself, you will find that extra help in the kitchen frees you to mingle with your guests, introduce them to other attendees, and tend to details like refilling drinks, checking on the food, and escorting guests to the door when the party ends.

Before you select a caterer, either from someone you've used before or a referral from a friend, you should first work out the details of your event including date, time, number of guests, type of party, timeline, and budget. You also should have an idea of the types of food to serve. When you meet with the caterer to present your party plans, meet at the location of the party so the caterer will know what kind of space they have to work with. You should discuss what services you want the caterer to provide. Do you want them to cook and serve food or do you want them to greet guests, hang coats, and bar tend? If you will need to rent tables, chairs, and linens, or extra plates and glassware, then you also should discuss whether the caterer will handle that for you. The caterer should also inspect the kitchen at this time. After the initial meeting, the caterer will put together a few sample menus with a price per person estimate. When you decide on the menu and the responsibilities of the caterer, review and sign the contract, check in a week before the event and, once again, on the day before. When the caterer arrives for the event, keep guests out of the kitchen, so they can complete the job they have been hired to do.

Guests with Allergies

When guests call and RSVP, particularly for a sit-down dinner party, you should ask if they have any dietary restrictions. Inquiring about this information is not as important with a cocktail or buffet party since you will serve a variety of dishes. If your guest does have a restriction, try to meet her needs. However, the host does not have to meet all of the dietary restrictions. If someone is particular, he or she should try to enjoy what you are serving or offer to bring his own dish. On the other hand, if the guest with the restrictions is the guest of honor, then the hostess should go above and beyond to accommodate that guest.

Potluck Parties

A potluck party is a smart way for the hostess to delegate some of the cooking to other friends. Usually, invited guests bring one of their favorite dishes, or one that they make very well, but the hostess can advise guests that she wants to follow a particular menu or type of food and ask guests to bring special dishes. A potluck also is a great source for new recipes.

Music, Flowers, and Decorations

Music adds a major element to any party, whether it's used for background ambience or to get the party really started. When only used for background, make sure that the music doesn't override the conversation. If your party will have plenty of dancing, then by all means, crank it up.

In terms of your selection, try a light music, such as jazz or classical for background music at a cocktail or dinner party. For a dancing event, use your own tastes and combine it with tastes of your guest to assemble your play list. If you are not hiring a DJ or a band, estimate the length of the party so that you can have the music ready and don't encounter a dead silence. You can always use CDs or make a playlist with a mixture of songs and, if necessary, play it more than once if the party ends up lasting longer than the music. At a smaller party, feel free to ask guests what songs they like and then do your best to accommodate them.

Flowers make the ultimate decorating statement. A bouquet or a large arrangement can add glamour to your festivities. If you don't have the decorating skills to put together an artful bunch, hire a professional florist. To save money, select flowers that are in season. When hiring a professional, consider a large bouquet of flowers for a centerpiece, and smaller arrangements in the powder rooms and living room. Consider adorning the entry way as well. The flowers will probably range from $100 for a larger arrangement to $25 for each small flower bouquet. If your party is buffet style, you may decorate the buffet table, but keep the floral arrangement small so that it is not a deterrent to reaching foods. If you decide to go the less expensive route and do-it-yourself, keep the arrangements very simple. Try bunches of one kind of flower, like sunflowers, daisies, or roses; cut the stems short and put them in short vases for easy arranging. Keep the flowers out of the heat to prevent them from wilting.

meagan says ...

Large dogs can be intimidating and sometimes guests have allergies to certain pets. To make sure all guests are comfortable, consider putting all pets in a closed-off area of your home before your company arrives.

Outdoor Parties

The great outdoors can be a fantastic setting for a party. If you are entertaining at home and weather permits, consider hosting some of the party outdoors on the deck or patio. Or, you can always decide to have the entire party outside. There's nothing like a party with the stars peeking down at your guests. Of course, everyone crosses their fingers and hopes that Mother Nature will honor them with warm, sunny weather. The best thing to do, just in case Mother Nature doesn't hear you, is to have alternate plans. Your first option is to select an alternate date. This option might not be feasible if you are serving large amounts of food or have invested in a caterer and wait staff.

You also can secure a secondary location. The alternate site can be indoors at your home or another location. The best alternate site option is someplace close by so that the transition is not confusing to guests.

When planning an outdoor event and you have an alternate date or site, you should clearly note that information on the invitation. On the day of the party, check the weather and if there's a high chance of inclement weather, start moving the party to the alternate site. You also should start contacting guests to remind them of the alternate site. If you have a large guest list, enlist the help of friends to contact guests.

As with an indoor party, you need to get your checklist and determine a menu, number of guests, seating, and tables.

You also might want to consider renting a tent to protect guests from the sun and to add ambience to your party. With certain tents, if you get a small sprinkle rather than a downpour, your guests are protected and you can still keep the party outdoors.

Some tents have four sides, some have windows, and some only have a canopy. Determine the type of tent you need based on the type of party and the number of guests you will have.

To find out what's available, ask a friend for a referral or contact local tent rental companies. Consider whether you want a dance floor, lighting, heat, or air conditioning. Regardless of what kind you rent, most suppliers will set up the tent and also take it down. If you are planning your party during the height of wedding season, book your tent as soon as possible.

Last, even at an outdoor party, someone is going to need the powder room. Portable facilities have come a long way from the miniature outhouses you see near construction sites. Companies that rent portable toilets now have really nice "bathrooms" that have mirrors, sinks, and even more than one stall. So if you don't want guests in the house, consider renting facilities for the outdoors.

With an outdoor party in your own backyard, you should give your neighbors a heads up. Leave a note or talk to the neighbors on both sides of your home to let them know what time the party starts and ends. A great way to break the ice, especially if you don't know your neighbors very well, is to invite them to the party as well. This way, no one is surprised by the sounds of music or the swarm of cars on the block.

Party Fiascos

Sometimes, no matter how much we plan, things can still go wrong. So, what do you do about the guests who won't leave, or if a guest spills red wine on your carpet? Well, the first rule of thumb is "don't panic; mistakes can and will happen." Try not to appear upset and don't make a big deal about the mishap. When the hostess is able to brush off an embarrassing accident, everyone else can breathe a sigh of relief.

When the hostess is able to
brush off an embarrassing
accident, everyone else can
breathe a sigh of relief.

Spills

If someone spills something, briefly take the time to clean up the spill and keep the party going. If someone spills something at the table, do not remove any plates or table settings or spend a lot of time cleaning up. Simply place napkins over the spot and keep the food coming. Likewise, if your carpet or furniture is stained, do not break out with the stain remover. Dab, wipe quickly, and keep it moving. You can tend to the stain more thoroughly after your guests leave.

If your guest breaks something, follow the same protocol for a spill. Do not look distressed and clean up quickly. A word of caution: If you have a vase or rug or anything else that is of value, monetary or emotional, consider putting it away when you entertain.

Of course, a thoughtful and well-mannered guest should offer to replace or repair the item that was damaged. When a guest insists on paying, you may give her an estimate of the cost or demur instead. If a guest doesn't offer anything, you should not push the issue, but you might reconsider whether to invite that guest back.

Guests Who Won't Leave

Sometimes you have a wonderful party and your guests don't want to leave. Despite how long the party has been going on, they are clearly not going anywhere. You can try a few nonverbal hints such as turning up the lights, serving coffee, or even clearing the tables. If that doesn't work, you can be very clear and inquire out loud about the time. When someone responds with the time, feign surprise and then announce that you have to get up early and start ushering people toward the door. The ever-classy Jackie Kennedy, well known for her White House parties, and her husband Jack did not believe in stopping a party that was still going strong. If they were tired, they would excuse themselves and allow their guests to party the night away. That's always another option if you're comfortable with leaving guests behind.

Intoxicated Guests

When a guest has too much to drink, the hostess must first of all try to minimize embarrassment for herself and other guests. Second, and most importantly the host must prevent the guest from getting behind the wheel of the car. As the host, you can be held legally liable if your guest ends up in accident.

When you see a guest getting tipsy, you can pull him to the side and offer him a cup of coffee. If the guest is past tipsy and becomes belligerent, angry, or sick, get the guest to a room and have him lie down. If the guest came to the party with someone, you and that guest can make sure someone else drives him home. If necessary, your guest might have to stay the night.

Uninvited Guests

Surprise! One of your guests showed up to your party with a friend in tow. As a graceful hostess you should warmly welcome the guest and prepare for the extra person. Usually this isn't a problem at a buffet or cocktail party. A dinner party, however, makes it more difficult to accommodate an extra person. If you are hosting a dinner party, quickly divide the foods as evenly as possible (even if this means slicing your steaks or chicken) and include the extra guest. Do not give up your plate since that will make the other guests, especially the uninvited guest, uncomfortable. Also, when the opportunity is available, tell your friend that you'd prefer advance notice the next time your guest brings an extra friend.

We've all been there before: a guest shows up with uninvited children in tow. As a host, when inviting guests for an adult-only function, you can informally call up your friend and say, "Do you think you'll be able to find a babysitter on Friday night?" That way your friend knows that you are only prepared to host adults at your function.

For a more formal function—one where an invitation is mailed—guests should know that the person invited to a function is the person whose name appears on an envelope. This is especially true with weddings. So, if you receive an invitation addressed simply to you, then please assume that you are the only invitee.

Of course, real life steps in and there will be times when a guest has an unexpected, out-of-town visitor or a babysitter who becomes suddenly sick. What to do then? Instead of showing up with the children or long-lost

cal says ...

It's always nice to bring a gift for the host or hostess of a party. Gourmet coffee or tea, a bottle of wine, or a book are all appropriate hostess gifts. When your guests bring you a food gift you are under no obligation to serve it. Thank your guest and tell them that you will enjoy the food. Your guest should present the food gift and advise that they hope you enjoy it later, which means that you both understand that the hostess will not serve the food during the evening.

college buddy, the guest should contact the host and ask if it's alright to attend the event with an uninvited guest. The hostess can advise whether the extra attendee will be welcomed. In the case of a child attending an event, the host might want to have a few reliable, trustworthy babysitter referrals available if some parents find themselves in a bit of pinch.

Of course, you can't please everyone. There are some parents that simply can't bear the thought of not taking their children everywhere with them. If a host encounters one of these loving parents who is offended by an adults-only affair, the host can explain the reasons why children are not invited. The host can say that the function was coordinated for a certain amount of people or that inviting children will take the host over budget. When confronted with a situation such as this, the host should be gracious with an explanation, but firm.

Last-Minute Cancellations

If you have to cancel or reschedule an event, try to contact all guests as soon as possible to inform them of the change. If time permits, send a notice through the mail. If not, call *and* e-mail everyone on your guest list. If the event will be rescheduled, let your guests know that when you make the call. To be sure everyone gets the message, make sure you get a response e-mail back or speak to an adult on the phone.

As you can see, a lot goes into planning a party. However, a little bit of organization goes a long way. The most important thing to remember is that once the event arrives, remember the purpose of the party—to mix with your guests, and to have fun.

wedding decorum

The next evening, I was on my way to meet Cal and Anissa for dinner. After all the hard work that I put into my cocktail party, I was ready to have a low-key night with my two best girlfriends.

Walking into the restaurant, I peered over the crowd to see if my girls were still waiting for a table. I couldn't see them, so I pulled out my cell phone. Before I could dial, I felt a tap on my shoulder and turned around to see Cal with a huge smile on her face. *Why is she so happy?* I wondered.

"Our table is in the back," she said, grabbing my hand. "You know Anissa was upset with the location and the view, but I was too hungry to argue. Follow me."

Cal weaved through the tables and I followed her, with a few excuse me's and pardon me's before we got to the table.

After I hugged Anissa hello and settled in, Cal piped up. "I have some wonderful news to share," she said, smiling and clapping her hands.

Before either one of us had a chance to guess what the news could be, she practically screamed, "Jimmy and I are getting married!" Look!"

As Cal threw her hand in my face, the ring drew my breath away. It was simple and elegant, like Cal. The Marquis-shaped diamond was a nice size, with two small diamonds on each side.

Cal started reciting the romantic engagement story and when she finished up, she grabbed both of our arms and said, "I want both of you to be in my wedding. Anissa, will you be my maid of honor?"

After we both happily agreed, Cal continued. "Oh yeah, I want to plan the wedding and be married in about three months, so this will *not* be a long process. I'll decide the date when we know what location is available."

"Three months!" I exclaimed. "I'm glad I don't have to go on a diet to fit in my dress." I laughed.

"We better get started," she said with a chuckle of pure happiness.

After that, I turned my attention to my menu. After all the excitement, I couldn't even think about food. It didn't matter though. Any feelings of hunger had been pushed aside. My best friend was getting married. And I was going to stand right there with her. ❧

Planning your wedding will be one of the most exciting events you will ever experience. Start by thinking about what kind of wedding you want to have and how much money you plan to spend. Once you determine style and budget, all of your other decisions—formality of dress, invitations, location, and even your menu—will all correlate and complement each other.

Like everything else, proper wedding etiquette ensures sure that the bride and groom host a classy event. From the first step—the engagement party—to the last step—thank-you cards—this chapter will ensure that your wedding will be a polished and elegant occasion.

Making the Announcement

The first step to getting married (after saying "yes" of course) is to announce your engagement plans to each family. The parents of the bride-to-be and the future groom should always be told first. It's proper to tell the bride's family first. If your parents are divorced, then the mother of the bride-to-be is told first, then your father, and then the future groom's parents. Next, tell your closest family members and then your friends. If one or both members of the engaged couple has children, the children should always be the first to hear the news, even before the couple's parents. Give the children the opportunity to ask questions and freely express their emotions by talking to each child alone without the presence of the future stepparent.

Formal Announcement

After family and close friends are told of the wonderful news, some couples opt to announce their engagement in the local paper. It is not protocol to mail engagement announcements, so the newspaper is the proper avenue to publicize the news if you wish to do so.

Typically, the bride's parents make the announcement, which can include the names of the bride, groom, and their parents; the wedding date; and education and job information about the couple. Usually, announcements will appear in the paper a few weeks before the wedding date, but for some newspapers with a widely read society/wedding page, the announcement could take months and might end up in the paper after the actual wedding date. An announcement could look like this:

The engagement of Veronica Caldwell to Mr. Donovan Rose, a son of Mr. and Mrs. David Rose of Detroit, has been announced by Mr. and Mrs. Miles Caldwell of Farmington Hills, Michigan, parents of the bride-to-be. Ms. Caldwell is a graduate of Clark University and is a social worker with the Pressley Lane agency. Mr. Rose is a graduate of Morehouse College and is a financial analyst with Cramer and Harris Accounting. The couple plans a summer wedding.

If the bride's parents are divorced, it could look like this:

Mrs. Jennifer Campbell announces the engagement of her daughter, Miss Tisha Stouffman. Miss Stouffman also is the daughter of Francis Hardaway . . .

If the groom's parents are divorced, the announcement could read:

Mr. and Mrs. Eddie Sanderson announce the engagement of their daughter, Miss Mailaka Sanderson, to Mr. Emil LaCrosse, son of Mrs. Christina Engelsdorf (of Atlanta, Georgia) and Mr. Alex McCain (of Buckhead, Georgia.) . . .

meagan says ...

One word of caution: Do not invite anyone to the engagement party that you won't invite to the wedding. Also, gifts are not expected at the engagement party.

After you inform your family and friends of the happy news, you can tell your coworkers in whatever manner you see fit—by announcing it a meeting, telling everyone individually, or telling a few people and letting word of mouth take care of the rest.

After everyone knows your wonderful news, the next step is to have an engagement party if you decide that you want one. The party can be formal or informal and includes the parents and also close family and friends. Ideally, the wedding attendants are present. Anyone can host the engagement party, but typically the bride's family, the groom's family, or even a close family friend hosts the event.

Paying for the Big Day

Before anyone starts to make arrangements for the wedding day, both families should decide who is paying for what expenses. If the bride and the groom will pay for their own wedding, the two of them should decide how to divide the expenses.

Tradition calls for the bride's family to pay for the majority of the expenses. Typically, the groom's party pays for the rehearsal dinner, the clergy fee, the bride's bouquet and usher's boutonnieres, the purchase of the wedding license, and the honeymoon. The rest is paid for by the bride's family.

Today's bride and groom are often older and gainfully employed, so many times they pay for the wedding themselves. If families decide to chip in, the bride and groom should sit down with the interested parties to discuss plans and a budget. The bride and the groom should first meet separately with both sets of parents and discuss all of the wedding expenses. Then, together, the families can decide who will pay for what. After everything is agreed upon, the couple should hand out a copy of the expense list for everyone to refer to during the wedding process. If the bride's or groom's family advises that they can't afford to help, the bride and the groom must work around their existing budget.

Selecting the Bridal Party

Old folklore says that the custom of selecting attendants to witness the marriage ceremony was to prevent evil spirits that were jealous of the bride's happiness from casting an evil spell on her. Then, tradition mandated that the bride walked to her wedding surrounded by her attendants, all dressed exactly like the bride, so the spirit wouldn't know which one was the bride.

Today, wedding attendants are not chosen to ward off evil spirits but to support the bride when it comes to planning one of the most important days of her life. And, just like the bride and groom have expenses to consider when planning a wedding, the wedding party has expenses as well. Bridal attendants are expected to pay for their own dress and shoes, at the very least. The financial responsibilities can be expanded to include their own lodging for the wedding night, the cost of a bachelorette party, bridal shower, and more, such as travel arrangements. Keep that in mind when asking out-of-town friends to stand in your wedding.

Selecting the bridal party can be fun but a bit tricky—especially if you stood in a friend's wedding, but you don't plan to ask her to stand in your wedding. Ultimately, the decision is up to you. However, because of the financial costs involved, you should give the wedding party as much advance notice as possible, just in case you need to select alternates.

When choosing your attendants, you should first consider close family and friends. Also keep in mind those closest to you who you deem to be especially helpful and supportive. Weddings can be stressful and you will certainly need plenty of assistance from family and friends (not to mention the groom).

If choosing your attendants becomes difficult and you are concerned with hurt feelings from those who were not asked to be an attendant, one way to resolve this is to ask them to act as a hostess or read a poem or Bible scripture at the ceremony. Once you decide on your attendants, you can continue to plan your wedding, but you should keep them informed of the plans. A letter or an e-mail that introduces the wedding party to each other and includes pertinent information is especially helpful.

The introductory letter could include:

- Date and location of the wedding
- List of names, addresses, e-mail addresses, and phone numbers of the wedding attendants
- Wedding rehearsal location and time
- Wedding rehearsal dinner location
- Lodging suggestions for out-of-town attendees
- Date of the bridal shower
- Prewedding photo arrangements
- Directions to the ceremony location

The Role of the Bridesmaids

On the bride's side, the wedding party usually consists of a maid (an unmarried woman) or matron (a married woman) of honor and bridesmaids. However, you can have a male honor attendant if you choose, and the groom can have a lady as his honor attendant.

Bridesmaids, especially the maid of honor, typically have many responsibilities surrounding the big day. Before the wedding, the bridesmaids arrange the bachelorette party and sometimes host the bridal shower. On the wedding day, the bridesmaids assist the mother of the bride with whatever tasks are at hand, such as helping the bride get dressed and welcoming guests.

The maid or matron of honor also has prewedding responsibilities. Typically, she helps the bride with the invitations and favors, helps her select her dress (if the bride requests help), coordinates the shower, and keeps records of the shower and wedding gifts.

During the wedding ceremony, the maid or matron of honor arranges the bride's train and veil at the altar, gives the bride the groom's ring at the appropriate time during the ceremony, and holds the bride's bouquet while the bride exchanges the vows. She also signs the wedding certificate as a witness to the nuptials. At the wedding, the maid or matron of honor can also toast the new couple.

The Guest List

Deciding who to invite to your wedding is often as difficult as selecting the perfect dress.

Above all, your guest list should accommodate your budget. After you, your groom, and the parents compile a "wish list," the next step is to start paring down the list to a reasonable number. One way to do this is to combine the lists and then take out certain categories of people (such as work associates, book club members, and distant cousins and relatives). If you place those people on a secondary list, you can still send invitations to some of them four weeks in advance—after guests on your primary list send their regrets.

The prospective bride and groom should agree on a number of invited guests. Although some invited guests will decline the invitation, you should still expect most of them to attend the wedding.

Remember that shower guests and those who attend the engagement party are always to be invited to the wedding. The one exception is when your coworkers give you an office shower. They do not have to be invited.

Invitations

Your invitation is the first way to communicate to guests what type of affair your wedding will be. If your wedding is informal, like a beach wedding that requires swimsuits and bikinis, then a casual invitation is appropriate. A formal wedding calls for a more refined invitation.

To simplify the wedding invitation you can exclude the groom's parents' names, especially if they are not heavily involved with the wedding planning.

The proper wording of a formal invitation is as follows:

> *Mr. and Mrs. John Olberman request the honor of your presence at the marriage of their daughter, Rachel Eliza, to Mr. Samuel Alan on Saturday, the fourth of June*
>
> *at four o'clock*
>
> *Russell Street Missionary Baptist Church*
>
> *Detroit, Michigan*

If the bride and groom are paying for the wedding, a less formal example is:

> *Mackenzie Lyndsey Smith and Elijah Raymond Green request the pleasure of your company at their marriage Saturday, April 21, 2008, at two o'clock*
>
> *Greenfield Peace Lutheran Church*
>
> *Chicago, Illinois*

If you are having your reception at a different location than where you are married, you should include a reception card with your invitation. This is especially important if you are not inviting every guest to the reception; in that case, then only include reception information in the invitation for those guests. It's nice if you can afford to invite every guest, but if you have a budget, you will have to limit the number of attendees.

The card should include the name and address of the locale with "Reception immediately following the ceremony" at the top of the card.

Your reception card should tell your guests whether you are having a meal by indicating "Dinner Reception" or "Luncheon Reception." If you are not planning a meal, use the wording "Cocktail Reception."

RSVP Cards

To manage the number of guests who attend your reception, you should include an RSVP card. The RSVP card should be mailed already stamped, so that guests can simply drop the response card in the mail. Guests check "accept," along with the number of people attending, or "regret" and mail the reply card in the envelope provided. If you are providing more than one option for a meal, the response card should have the options listed and a space for guests to indicate which meal they would like.

Assembling, Addressing, and Mailing Your Invitations

While all wedding invitations should include the invitation and reply card, in some cases, a reception card, an outer envelope, and tissue paper are also included.

The invitation should be assembled as follows:

- ∞ The outer envelope is sealed and contains the inner envelope, unsealed and placed with the guest's name face up.
- ∞ The tissue can be used to cover your invitation.
- ∞ The items are placed in the inner envelope in order of importance, beginning with the invitation. Then the reply card is tucked under the flap of the reply envelope, followed by a reception card and any other card (directions or travel accommodations) that you wish to include.

It is best to keep wording formal. While it can feel odd to do so, the following rules should be followed when addressing the envelopes:

- ∞ Spell out words such as street, road, avenue, and boulevard.
- ∞ Use full names, even if they go by "Mike" instead of "Michael."
- ∞ Write out numbers one to twenty. Larger numbers can be written numerically.
- ∞ If a guest's name includes "Junior" or "Senior," this should be used on the outside mailing envelope but not on the inner.
- ∞ Do not use labels for the invitation envelopes. All of the envelopes should be handwritten. The bride and groom can address them or they can ask someone who has a beautiful handwriting or a calligrapher to do the honors. If using a professional calligrapher, the standard pay is one dollar an envelope.

Changing the Wedding Date

Sometimes an unforeseeable situation arises and the date of the wedding must be moved. If the wedding date changes after invitations are printed but before they are mailed, the bride can enclose a note advising the new date. The note might read, "The date of the wedding has been changed from April 21 to May 10." If invitations have been mailed, the bride can mail a card with a note, e-mail a note, or telephone guests advising them of the new date.

Registering for Gifts

Registering for gifts is a way to ease the stress of your guests selecting gifts they hope you will like and ensure you will like the gifts they give. When making selections for your wedding registry, make sure you include a wide range of prices. There is no rule that says a couple has to register for silver, china, and crystal. Feel free to register at locations that specialize in things having to do with your hobbies. A do-it-yourself, fishing, or even a camping store can stand in for the traditional registry.

Note that wedding registry information should not be included in the invitation. The bride and groom should spread the word to their parents and to the wedding attendants. The couple can give parents and the

anissa says …

Note to guests: The inner envelope states exactly who is invited to the wedding. If the inner envelope says "Richard and Cassandra Tucker," then both are invited. If the inner envelope says, "Brianna Richardson," then only Brianna is invited. If the inner envelope does not include the words "and Guest," then the invited person should only RSVP for herself.

maid of honor a list of stores where they registered so that they can share the news with guests. If guests want registry information, they should ask the bride, groom, parents, or a member of the wedding party.

The Receiving Line

After the wedding ceremony, the bride and groom, their parents, and key members of the wedding party often meet and greet every guest in a receiving line. Some newlyweds prefer to hold the receiving line at the reception hall before the festivities. The traditional order, which is based on the custom of the bride's parents assuming the costs of the wedding, is the following: The bride's mother and father are first in line to greet guests, followed by the mother and father of the groom, the bride and groom, maid of honor, and sometimes the bridesmaids. The bride and groom may forgo a receiving line, but it does give everyone the opportunity to greet most of the guests.

When divorced parents are standing in the receiving line, they do not stand together. The parent and stepparent who are giving the reception should stand in the line. If none of the parents have remarried and both have pitched in toward the cost of the reception, then both parents should stand in the line. When both couples have remarried and have helped give the wedding, the receiving line would look like this: bride's mother and stepparent, groom's mother and stepparent, bride's father and stepparent, groom's father and stepparent, bride, groom, maid of honor.

Bridesmaids can stand in the receiving line, but when the line is really long, they don't have to stand with the bride. Young wedding attendants do not stand in the receiving line, but children of the bride or groom can stand in the line if they are old enough to do so. Guests should offer a "congratulations" and move through the line. The only gift that should be given in a receiving line is an envelope, handed to the bride.

Gifts for the Wedding Party

It is customary for the bride and groom to give a small token to the wedding attendants. The maid of honor and the best man can be given more expensive gifts or the same gift as the wedding party. The bride can present the gifts to her wedding attendants at the bridal shower or at the rehearsal dinner. The groom also gives his gifts at the rehearsal dinner.

In addition to a shower gift, sometimes bridal attendants give a joint gift to the bride and the groomsmen give a joint gift to the groom. However, because it is costly to participate in a wedding party, this isn't necessary. Instead, the gift is simply standing in the wedding.

Wedding Favors

Although many companies supply personalized wedding favors, the favor is not a mandatory part of the wedding checklist. Favors can range from personalized boxes of chocolates, mini bottles of wine, or even monogrammed matches. Although they are quite lovely, they are not necessary except as a part of cultural tradition.

Thank-You Notes

Thank-you notes should be sent out to guests within four to six weeks of receiving the gift. The maximum amount of time for wedding thank-you notes is three months. These can be written on any kind of stationery or note cards immediately after the gift arrives.

Written notes are required and should always mention the specific gift and what you plan to do with it. Even if you don't like the gift, describe it as having a "unique personality" or even eclectic, but never let on that you dislike the gift. If possible, try to remember to display it when the gift giver comes to visit.

A printed note of thanks with no personal message added is inappropriate. Even if the words "thank you" already are printed on the stationery, a personal note should still be included.

General Guest Responsibilities

From the moment you receive a wedding invitation, you have commitments and responsibilities. As a guest, it's time for you to remember your

By keeping your manners intact and your host's feelings in mind, you are sure to be a guest that people will want at their functions again and again.

manners and be on your best behavior at the events surrounding the wedding. Just as the bride and groom have responsibilities, so do the invited guests.

Accept or Decline

The first responsibility you have as a wedding guest or invitee is to respond to the wedding invitation as soon as possible, especially if you cannot attend. A fast response allows the bride and groom to send out other invitations, if they have additional guests that they would like to invite. The prompt response also allows the couple to plan accordingly and determine the number of guests sooner than later.

Gifts

Guests who are invited to the ceremony and reception are expected to send a gift to the couple even if they can't attend. The only time this doesn't hold true is when an announcement of a marriage is sent out after the wedding has already taken place. The announcement can be acknowledged with a congratulatory note or card. If you are invited to a wedding and the couple requests a charitable donation in lieu of a gift, you should respect the couple's wishes.

No Thank-You Card Received

If three months have passed and you have not received a note of thanks, it is acceptable to ask the bride or groom if they received the gift. It's possible that the gift was separated from the card and the bride and groom have no idea who to thank. If the newlyweds have not received the gift, you can look into tracking it if it was mailed or opt to replace it.

You Can No Longer Attend the Wedding

If a conflict arises after you have sent an RSVP, you should call the bride as soon as possible, to let her know that you will no longer be able to attend. As stated before, you are still obligated to send a gift.

Proper Decorum, Please

Best behavior is mandatory for everyone at the wedding. The ceremony is not the time to crack jokes about, or even mention, ex-boyfriends or girlfriends (or ex-husbands or wives). Everyone should be polite and conduct themselves appropriately. The wedding is about the bride and the groom and their new beginning. Everyone should remember that.

During the Wedding Ceremony

At the church or place where the wedding ceremony will take place, try to keep mingling to a minimum. Talking once the ceremony has started also should be limited. Often the wedding officiant will advise whether taking pictures during the ceremony is permitted. If not allowed, you should refrain from taking pictures. If pictures are allowed, be respectful and give the wedding photographer the opportunity to snap photos first. Never block the view of other guests while trying to take photos.

If the ceremony is conducted under a religious denomination that is not the same as your own, participate in all aspects you are comfortable with. When the other guests stand or sit, you should do the same. You do not have to recite prayers that contradict your own religion or beliefs.

During the Reception

Although things can get livelier at the reception, guests still should not take the excitement too far. Keep in mind that while there may be dancing, music, and an open bar, it is still a wedding and the biggest day of the bride's and groom's lives.

When in the receiving line at the church or at the reception hall, greet the bride and groom briefly and keep the line moving. You can say something like "Congratulations. I am so happy for you." The bride and groom will appreciate your brevity and will be able to greet all of the guests in a timely manner and move on to the celebration.

After the Reception Ends

Beautiful centerpieces are part of a reception. After the reception ends, you should not assume that they will be disposed of and freely take them home. Unless the new couple encourages guests to take them, they should be left in the center of the table. It is possible that the couple has asked members of the bridal party to take the centerpieces or even decided to donate them to a local church or soup kitchen. Also, never ask for doggie bags if you haven't finished your meal.

Even keeping all this in mind, unexpected circumstances can leave you wondering how to handle yourself like an ideal guest. Here are situations that you might encounter as a guest—and how to handle them like a pro.

The cost of being a wedding attendant is proving to be expensive.
Whenever you accept a role in a wedding, you are undertaking quite
a few expenses, including travel and hotel accommodations if you live
out of town. If you are asked to stand in a wedding but know that the
commitment will create a financial strain, you should politely decline
the invitation and honestly explain that you can't afford the expenses.
The bride or groom can either find a less taxing role for you or offer to
pay for your expenses. If the bride or groom does pay for your wedding
expenses, no one else in the wedding party needs to know about the
agreement.

**You have agreed to be a wedding attendant but can no longer partici-
pate.** While it is unfortunate, occasionally you may need to bow out of
your role as a wedding attendant. If this happens, the most important
thing is to alert the bride as soon as you know you won't be able to participate. It will be up to the bride and groom to decide if they want to
enlist the aid of a replacement bridal attendant.

You are invited to the wedding as a single guest. If you receive a wedding invitation addressed only to you, you should presume that you are
invited to the wedding on your own. Unless you get engaged or reunite
with an estranged spouse, the bride and groom do not have to invite
your significant other. It is considered impolite for an invited guest to
ask if they can bring a guest to the wedding. However, it is not impolite
for the bride or groom to refuse the additional person.

wedding decorum

133

No babysitter/children at the wedding. Just as the wedding invitation clearly states who is invited to the wedding, if your children's names are not on the envelope, then they are not invited. If you run into problems getting a babysitter, resist the urge to ask the bride and groom if you can bring your child. Again, it is considered impolite to ask to bring an extra guest to a wedding, even if it's a child. Once the couple has decided that children will not be invited, they must not make an exception for one guest to avoid hurt feelings among other guests. You can, however, reach out to other wedding guests who have children and ask them what their childcare arrangements are. Perhaps your child can be included in this arrangement. If this happens, be sure to thank the parent who is sharing his or her babysitter, and pay for your child's share of the babysitting fee.

You are able to attend the ceremony but not the reception. Sometimes a guest will not be able to attend the ceremony and the reception or vice versa. If this is the case for you, you should write your response on the RSVP card and indicate which event you will attend. If you can only attend the ceremony, that leaves room for the bride and groom to invite someone else to the reception.

Weddings are a joyous occasion. By keeping your manners intact and your host's feelings in mind, you are sure to be a guest that people will want at their functions again and again.

CHAPTER 8

baby showers

Cal and Jimmy's engagement wasn't the only thing that turned out to be whirlwind. Precisely three months after their honeymoon, the happy couple announced that they were expecting a baby. As if the fact that my best friend was going to be a mommy wasn't thrilling enough, Cal took me out to dinner one night and asked me to be her baby's godmother. Of course, I accepted, and smiled to myself the whole way home.

Over the next few months, I took great pains to plan the perfect baby shower. Since we didn't know the sex of the baby and Cal used green in her wedding, I decided to have an all-white shower.

With the help of Cal's mother and a few close friends, I hosted the shower in Cal and Jimmy's backyard and everything went off without a hitch. Actually, there was a small hitch: Cal went into labor a few hours after the shower ended. At eight months and three weeks, we all were a little nervous, but twenty-two hours later little Chase arrived—and he was perfect.

Not exactly the type of ending we predicted for our classy bash, but none of us could think of a more perfect ending to a gathering of friends to celebrate Cal and her new arrival. ❧

When a good friend or family member is expecting a baby, you want to throw them a shower worthy of the thrilling news. This chapter will give you everything you need to know in order to host a classy but celebratory baby shower.

Baby Basics

Typically, baby showers are held for the mom-to-be's first baby. The shower is usually held near the end of the pregnancy, around the seventh or eight month. Showers held later than that will sometimes have a missing mom or a new baby in attendance. When the mother has had a difficult pregnancy, the shower can be held after the baby arrives.

The rules for shower invitations are similar to wedding invitations: Mail them out about six weeks in advance of the date. The invitation should include the following:

- ∞ Name of the guest of honor (the mom-to-be)
- ∞ Date and time
- ∞ Location
- ∞ Address of shower and a map
- ∞ RSVP date and phone number
- ∞ Shower theme (if applicable)
- ∞ Sex of the baby (optional)
- ∞ Host's name and phone number

If you are inviting a guest who has had a miscarriage or is having a difficult time conceiving, you may want to call her before sending an invitation. If she prefers not to attend, your call lets her know that you would like for her to attend but you understand if she decides not to.

Who Hosts?

Usually a good friend of the mom-to-be hosts the shower. In the past, it was considered inappropriate for a family member to give the shower, for fear of appearing to solicit gifts, but today it's common for the mom-to-be's family to help plan the shower.

Shower registry is never included in the invitation, because it's considered presumptuous to ask for gifts. Guests should ask the hosts where the mom-to-be is registered when they RSVP.

Guest List

Traditionally, only women attended showers. However, the mom-to-be might request a shower that includes men as well. Usually, family members of the mother and father-to-be and close friends are invited to the shower.

The host of the shower should consult with the mom-to-be to determine who to include on the guest list. The number of guests can range from an intimate affair to a larger bash. If the guest list seems too large, consider holding two showers in honor of the mom. One shower can be for friends and the other for family. Or, mix it up a little: Hold one shower for the mom-to-be's friends and family and the other for the dad-to-be's family and friends. Whatever you decide is fine.

Gifts and Registry

Gift registry information should not be included in the shower invitations. The parents-to-be are responsible for registering for the baby items they will need. The host is responsible for consulting with the mom-to-be so that when guests call to RSVP and ask for gift ideas, the host will have the list available to help guests determine what is needed for the new mother.

It is the host's responsibility to spread the word to the invited guests about the gift registry.

Menu for Showers

A baby shower menu can consist of all types of foods. The foods should be determined by the budget of the hostess, the time of day, and also coincide with the season.

If planning a buffet-style menu, the hostess can prepare (or have prepared) various types of foods so there will be plenty to choose from. Most importantly, buffet foods should be easy to enjoy without fear of sauces and gravies spilling.

If guests know the sex of the baby, menu items can be selected with a pink or blue theme. If the mother is expecting a baby girl, the foods can consist of a creamy tomato soup, which will have a slight pink tinge, salmon, or a pink dessert. Blue foods are a little more difficult to create, but blue-hued potatoes can serve as a side dish—blue corn chips, blueberries, and plums if the shower is held when the fruits are in season. Of course, the cake frosting or dessert also can be blue. Drinks can include pink lemonade or blueberry punch.

As with any party, your food and menu should reflect the time of day. For example, if you have a baby shower in the evening, heartier dinner foods would be more appropriate than brunch items.

Baby Shower Decorations

When the baby shower has a theme, decorations simply follow that idea. If the shower has no particular theme, then the host is not limited to any particular type of design or pattern. Decorations create a fun atmosphere and can be as simple or elaborate as the hostess likes. Flowers are always appropriate for a baby shower and the celebration of a birth.

Of course, the hostess should take the expectant mom's taste into consideration when deciding what kind of decorations to use. In addition to flowers, you could make a garland from photos of the mother and father's childhoods or a hanging mobile made of wooden alphabet blocks to hang over the buffet.

Baby Shower Games

Baby shower games are not a requirement, but most showers have some type of interaction among the guests. The best thing about games is that they allow guests to get to know each other in a fun way and increases the chances that two guests sitting on opposite sides of the room will have a chance to interact. Typically, if games are played, two or three games are introduced. The hostess should ask the expectant mom her preference. The mother-to-be can consider the guests who are attending when she makes her decision. Will most of the guests already know each other? Then perhaps games won't be needed to encourage conversation. If the new mom loves playing games, then she will certainly want games at her shower. Be aware that games that focus too much on the expectant mother (or her growing belly) may make her feel uncomfortable.

Baby Shower Favors

Giving guests a favor at a baby shower is a nice gesture. They can range from a decorative soaps, photo frames, packets of seeds, a candy bar, a miniature baby bottle filled with candy, or even pink and blue candles, all with the mom-to-be's name and the shower date printed on them. However, favors are not required, even though they are a fun idea. They can be a fun and inexpensive way to say thank-you to guests for attending the party. Remember that favors do not replace thank-you cards, which should still be mailed to all of your guests.

Showers with a Theme

Following a theme helps make decorating a shower easier for the hostess. You might decide that polka dots, daisies, or even a blue (or pink!) and white theme are nice themes for the shower. That doesn't mean that everything needs polka dots or daisies, but certainly the table linens, dessert, and the menu can coordinate with the theme.

Some ideas include the following:

THEMES FOR A *Baby Shower*

An "Around the Clock" shower: This theme calls for the party to revolve around a certain time of day. For example, if the shower takes place in the morning, you can serve breakfast foods and decorate with yellow and other colors associated with morning. Guests can bring gifts that relate to morning hours or books that include pictures of the sun. If the shower occurs in the evening, you can decorate with stars and moons, and guests can bring pajamas and books with a nighttime theme, such as lullabies or *Goodnight, Moon*.

"A Star is Born" shower: For this shower, the hostess can decorate with a Hollywood theme, even rolling out a red carpet where you can snap pictures of the guests as they arrive and videotape a special message to the mom-to-be.

A "Building Baby's Library" shower: This shower is a great idea if the mother-to-be would like guests to bring a new book for her impending arrival. She can register for the books that she would like for the baby, and you, as the host, can decorate around the theme of a certain book, such as *Winnie-the-Pooh* or *Pat the Bunny*.

Whatever theme you decide upon, be sure to discuss the idea with the mother-to-be so that you can be sure that she likes the theme and it reflects her personality.

Showers for Special Circumstances

A baby shower is always a special occasion. But sometimes these special occasions may involve even more unusual circumstances! The following section addresses everything you need to know if the baby shower is going to be an extraordinary affair.

Showers for Multiple Babies

These days, it's raining babies and some of your friends may be having two, three, or more babies at one time. As a guest, you don't have to buy an individual gift for each baby. Instead, consider purchasing one gift that the mother can use for all of the babies such as a basket full of diapers, a barrel of wipes, or a colorful selection of onesies.

Showers for an Out-of-Town Mom

If a friend is expecting a baby and lives out of town, you can still throw a pseudo shower for her by creating a shower in a box. You can invite other close friends of the new mom to contribute a gift. After receiving all of the gifts, you can mail the box of gifts to the out-of-town mom. When the expectant mom receives the box of gifts, she'll be pleasantly surprised and feel very loved.

Co-ed Baby Showers

Traditionally, women only attend showers, but today showers can be co-ed and include the father, his friends, family members, and other couples. As the hostess, you should ask the expectant mother if she would enjoy having a co-ed shower. Some guests-of-honor may not feel comfortable with a mixed shower, while others will want their husband to be the only man to attend. The shower is for the new mom, and ultimately the guest list is her decision.

Showers for Second Babies

Showers are usually held for the first baby, with friends and family realizing that a childless household will need to be completely overhauled for a new baby. Subsequent babies can be celebrated as well, but instead of a shower, the baby's family might organize a brunch or a dinner to introduce the new arrival to friends.

If friends decide to celebrate the new arrival, they can do so without calling it a shower, and also leave the idea of giving gifts rather vague. Mothers should not register for gifts so that those who already bought gifts for the first child don't feel obligated to buy a another one. If guests do bring the new baby a present, it's really nice to give the older children a small token as well so they won't feel left out of the festivities.

At a second (or third or fourth) baby celebration, the gifts are usually geared toward the new mom—spa gifts, certificates for home-delivered meals, and so on—rather than for the new baby.

One idea for a second baby celebration is to give the party a pampering theme. At a "Pamper Me" themed celebration, guests can give the new mother gift certificates for a massage or manicure, lounging clothes, and other luxurious gifts so that she can remember to pamper herself even while taking care of her new addition.

Another idea for a second-time mom is a "Deep Freezer" party where guests bring a cooked meal that can be frozen and later enjoyed when the new mother is too tired to cook meals for herself and family after the baby arrives.

Baby Showers for Adoptive Families

A shower is a great way to welcome an adopted baby into the family. When planning a shower for an adopted child, it's best to make sure that the adoption is final before selecting a date for the shower. Since the parents are getting acquainted with the new baby after bringing him or her home, the hostess should ask the new mom what shower date works best for her. The shower should be the same type of shower that a new mom would garner.

If the adopted child is older, a welcoming party, which is like a birthday party, is a better option than a traditional baby shower.

Visiting the New Addition

Once the new mom is at home with her baby and has had a chance to settle in, you should call her and ask the best day and time for you to visit. You can bring a gift for the baby, but if you have already given a shower gift, you are not obligated to give another one. A nice gesture is to take a prepared meal for the family since the new parents will be somewhat overwhelmed with their new baby. If the new mother is comfortable with you holding her precious baby, make sure you wash your hands first. Because infants put their hands in their mouths, you can decrease the spread of germs to the baby by trying not to touch the baby's hands. Keep your visit brief so that you do not tire out the new mother and baby or throw off their very sensitive schedule.

If the New Baby Has a Health Issue

New parents are overwhelmed with a new baby, and when the child has a disability or serious health condition, childcare can be even more challenging. To deal with the challenges ahead, the family needs support and love. If your friend has a child with a disability, words of encouragement, a gift, or even a listening ear all will help provide comfort. Most of all, be the best friend that you can be.

the art of
gift-giving

When Deanna called the team into the conference room to announce her pregnancy and to let us know that she would be missing a few days of work here and there—which was really the good news for her staff—it all made sense. After our meeting, a few of us gathered together and began making plans for a group gift to be presented to her at a baby shower.

Even though Deanna could be hard-nosed, I decided to buy her an additional gift strictly from me. I'd rather err on the side of doing *more* rather than doing nothing. I'm sure a few of my colleagues sneaked her a present too. My gift was a spa appointment that she could enjoy after she had the baby. I mailed it to her home rather than presenting it to her at the group shower, where she was touched by the group gift of a crib that we picked from her registry.

A few weeks after her baby shower (and a few days after the arrival of her baby), we received a thank-you note from Deanna:

Dear Team,

Thank you so much for the beautiful crib! I absolutely love it! The crib and bedding matches the nursery décor perfectly and Bianca loves her new bed. She is already too big for her bassinet so the crib suits her perfectly. Thank you again, team, for the wonderful gift. It was very thoughtful and kind of all of you. I will never forget your generosity.

Sincerely,
Deanna

That night, I received a personal thank-you card at my home.

Dear Meagan,

Thank you so much for the spa gift. You know I absolutely love a massage and tissue wrap. I plan to book an appointment right before I return to work. However, I want you to remember that it is inappropriate to give expensive gifts to your boss. The gift can be misconstrued as an attempt to gain favoritism or perks. Since I know that is not what you intended, please know that I am excited about my visit to Sabbatical Spa. I haven't been there before but I'm sure I'll enjoy it.

    Also, please continue to update Mr. Gale's schedule, travel arrangements, and interview calendar, and e-mail it to me every Friday by 10 A.M. Again, I appreciate your hard work and the spa gift.

Sincerely,
Deanna

When I showed the thank-you letter to Anissa, I told her I couldn't believe it. But to be honest, I was looking for a little favoritism. However, all it got me was another dressing down—in the unexpected format of a thank-you note. ❧

Giving gifts can be a scary prospect. Determining how much to spend, what to buy, and when a present is really necessary can be a daunting task. However, when a gift is necessary, there are a few guidelines to make the giving process easier and smoother.

When giving a gift, you have three responsibilities:

- ❧ You must choose something appropriate for the recipient.
- ❧ You must ensure the gift arrives on time if it is intended for an occasion.
- ❧ You must give the present freely with no strings attached. (that is, don't expect anything in return).

The recipient's only responsibility is to acknowledge the gift promptly with a handwritten thank-you note.

Quite often, you may get invited to an occasion where it is expected that guests bring a gift. These occasions include:

- ❧ Birthday parties
- ❧ Baby showers or your first visits to a new baby
- ❧ Housewarmings
- ❧ Retirements
- ❧ Weddings
- ❧ Bridal Showers

Giving Green

Sometimes you might wonder whether a monetary gift is appropriate or even expected. While this is a tricky question that has no definitive answer, occasions where money is often given as a gift include:

- ↶ Weddings
- ↶ Bar or bat mitzvahs
- ↶ High school or college graduations
- ↶ Retirement
- ↶ When an unexpected tragedy occurs that requires immediate funds

meagan says ...

Whenever you're not sure if you should bring a gift to an occasion, simply ask the host if other guests are bringing gifts and then follow suit.

Gifts at Work

As illustrated in the story at the beginning of the chapter, giving presents at work can be trickier than buying gifts for family and friends. It can be fun, but gifting at the office can be awkward and misconstrued.

If you are the boss, you should remember that you should gift everyone the same. If you buy one person a birthday gift, then you should buy everyone on your staff one. Depending on the size of your staff, that can be difficult. The best thing for a boss to do is participate in collections that go around the office. The only exception to this is when the boss gifts his or her administrative assistant. Because they often are the lifeline to the boss, their gift can be more substantial.

In many work settings, coworkers often contribute money for a group present. Try to contribute your fair share. You'd want people to contribute when the hat is passed for you. However, if you absolutely can't afford to chip in, tell the person collecting the money that you simply can't afford it and offer to help in another way. Perhaps you can do the legwork in going to purchase the gift, or make a snack to bring to the party.

Selecting the Right Gift

A gift is an offering that expresses your affection and regard for the recipient. It should reflect the recipient's tastes, not yours. Consider the person's interests and hobbies. Someone who likes poetry will probably love the newest book by a favorite poet. Likewise, a classical music lover will enjoy a CD and a regular coffee drinker will appreciate a gift of gourmet coffee. Here are suggestions for common gift-giving occasions:

- Baby shower gifts
  - Photo album or baby book
  - Engraved silver cup or spoon
  - Baby-sitting services
  - Anything off the new mom's gift registry

ॐ Christening, baptism, bris, or secular naming ceremony gifts
- A personalized Bible
- Gold or silver cross or Star of David for a necklace or a charm bracelet
- Biblical bookmark
- An outfit for the baby
- Something from the baby's gift registry

ॐ Graduation gifts
- Money, which is especially appreciated if the student is college bound
- Luggage for a graduate going to college or a briefcase for one entering the work force
- A book about the new city where the student will attend school
- Dictionary and thesaurus
- Gift certificate to a store that sells school supplies and dorm room accompaniments
- Prepaid cell phone to call home from college

ॐ Gifts for people who are ill, recovering, or can't get out much
- Books on tape
- Magazines or a magazine subscription
- Homemade foods that can be easily prepared or heated
- Fruit basket
- Portable CD player and CDs
- Offer to check in on the family at home with cooked meals

- Offer to run errands
- Fragrant soaps and lotions
- Movies

∿ Gifts for new or first-time home owners
- Cookbooks
- Plants
- Kitchen accessories and new cooking tools
- Home-cooked meal
- Subscription to a home décor magazine
- Offer to help unpack boxes
- Gift certificate to the local do-it-yourself store

∿ Birthday of a close friend
- Brunch, lunch, or dinner for the two of you
- Homemade dessert
- Perfume
- Book by her favorite author; a signed copy is even better
- Pamper-me gift basket with soaps, oils, and lotions
- CDs from her favorite artist
- Spa visit
- Flowers

∿ Retirement gifts
- A gift certificate to a favorite restaurant
- A signed memento from all of the coworkers
- Photo album with pictures from various events that the retiree was a part of

- Gifts related to his or her special interests or hobbies
- Money
- A group picture of the retiree's friends at the office

Presenting Your Gift

Always try to present your gift no later than the day of the event. A late gift is okay, but it's best to give the gift on time. If you are out of town, mail the present so that it arrives on the day of the event. If you send your gift late, enclose a note apologizing for the tardiness.

meagan says ...

As tempting as it may be, it is never appropriate to "re-gift." Your faux pas could easily be discovered if the person asks to exchange the gift, or if he or she mentions, wears, or displays the present in front of the original gifter. More importantly, when someone gives you a gift, he or she has presumably put time, effort, and money toward giving you a thoughtful present. Giving this gift to someone else and passing it off as a new item is callous. Rather than giving away the gift, you could make the extra effort to wear or display the gift when in the company of the person who gave it to you. Your friend is sure to appreciate it.

Receiving Gifts

Gifts should be opened when you receive them unless the event is huge, like a wedding or a large party. You should be equally enthusiastic while opening all presents.

the art of gift-giving

Expressing Thanks for a Gift

Always express thanks immediately upon receiving a gift. If the giver is there in person, express your thanks and say something specific about the gift, like what you plan to do with the gift or how you will display the gift. If a gift is received by mail, pick up the phone and express thanks right away.

Even if you thank the person face-to-face or over the phone, you must send a handwritten note. E-mails are not acceptable, nor is handing out prewritten thank-you notes at the end of an event.

Thank-you notes should include the following:

- A specific reference to the gift
- A sincere expression of gratitude
- An indication of how you will use the gift
- An appropriate closing sentiment

While writing a thank-you note for a monetary gift, you should describe how you plan to use the money.

Gift giving is certainly one of the small joys in life, and you shouldn't let worries of committing a social faux pas take away from the event. When bestowing a gift, be sure to keep golden rule of giving in mind (always give a gift without expecting anything in return), and you are sure to have a mutually pleasant experience.

social grace in the workplace

On Friday, I went out with coworkers to have a few drinks and unwind from a busy week at work. We ended up at Olive, a new martini bar. Like all work parties, the gossip was flowing as quickly as the drinks.

I found out that Keith was leaving the department for a six-month overseas position. Once the gossip dried up at the table where I was sitting, I stored the new job info in my somewhat tipsy brain and kept it moving to the next group of people. At the second table, Fredrique and Charlotte had their heads close together, whispering, and their body contact struck me as a little odd. Maybe a little more comfortable than two coworkers should be. Still, I shrugged it off and moved to another group for one last drink before heading home for the night.

When I walked into the office on Monday, I could tell that something was amiss. I walked by a huddle of people standing outside the suite looking very intense. So, with my coffee cup in hand so I wouldn't look too obvious, I walked over to them and greeted everyone. Paul, a former news anchor who always has the scoop whenever there is one, beckoned me over and asked if I had heard what happened at the lounge on Friday.

He was whispering, so I started whispering too. "No, I haven't heard anything. What happened?"

"Charlotte got fired this morning," said Paul.

"Charlotte?" I repeated. "For what? What happened?" Charlotte was pretty well liked in our department and for her to get fired meant that something pretty serious had occurred. Something that nobody could brush off regardless of how popular she was.

"Did you see her at Olive on Friday?" asked Paul. "She was really toasted—she had way too much to drink. So, when the band starts playing, she jumps up on the table and starts dancing provocatively and screaming at the top of her lungs."

"Oh no," I said in disbelief. I knew where this was going.

Kyria piped in and said "Yeah, and the band started egging her on. Everyone was looking. Some people were laughing and clapping, but everyone that was still there from work was horrified."

"I didn't know what to do so I asked the waitress for my bill so that I could get out of there, but then I realized that she probably needed a ride home, so I waited for her to stop dancing," said Paul.

"Well, how long did that take?" I asked.

"Two songs and boy were they long songs," said Paul. "When she finally got off the table, I got her purse and told her it was time to leave. On our way out, people gave her a standing ovation. I was so embarrassed."

"How did Marcie find out?"

"When I got here this morning, Marcie walked to my desk and asked if she could meet with me. She asked me all about it, but she already knew what happened," said Kyria.

"She called me in too and when we finished talking she gave me a code of conduct booklet and told me that Charlotte was no longer employed here," said Paul. "I knew that she knew what happened when she asked me to come to her office. I've never even had a conversation with her."

"Wow," I said. "That is something. Just think what could have happened if you hadn't driven her home."

"Yeah. I wonder who told Marcie," said Paul. "We'll probably never know."

With that, I filled my coffee cup and headed back to my desk. ❧

Your personal life and your life at work are often two separate entities, and most of the time it's best that way. Networking and office politics are all part of moving up the corporate ladder, which means getting to know your colleagues and maybe finding a mentor. The office is the place where you are always professional and on your best behavior. Office hours and work-related social gatherings are not the time for you to complain about your boyfriend, your boss, or other colleagues. Leave those conversations to your friends outside of work and stay focused on remaining professional—even if you're not officially on the clock.

Office Parties

Inevitably, the time comes when your department or entire workplace is hosting a work function. It might be the annual team-building summer event or the holiday party. Even if you don't like your colleagues, you're looking for another job, or you have a real conflict, you should make every effort to attend. Usually nobody will say that attendance is mandatory, but people notice when someone is absent.

Attending a party with your coworkers is different from partying with your friends in several ways—dress, conversation, alcohol consumption, and politics.

First, you must always dress professionally even if the event is a picnic and it's hotter than July. Wear demure clothing that still fit the occasion. Shorts are fine, but make sure they are at least mid-thigh or knee

Often the office party gives you the opportunity to network, interact, and possibly meet an executive or higher-up that you never encounter during regular workdays. You should take the opportunity to meet the executive and introduce yourself. You should not inquire about a job in the executive's department or use the conversation to talk about policies that you don't like and would like to see change.

length. Instead of a halter or a cropped shirt, wear a modest T-shirt with no political statements.

If the party is at night and requires evening wear, make sure your neckline isn't plunging, your dress isn't too tight, or your jewelry too ostentatious. Keep in mind that an office party doesn't mean that you can drop your guard and dress as if you were hanging out with friends.

Avoid overindulging—or even better—indulging in alcohol at the office party. You don't want to give the appearance that you are inebriated.

Don't forget that office politics are still evident at any office event. Always remain professional and use the party as the opportunity to greet everyone and meet others you don't know. When thinking of safe topics of conversation, sports, music, or movies are always good conversation builders, since these are light, noncontroversial subjects. Stay away from religion, politics, or gossiping about people at work.

Dating in the Workplace

Most companies frown upon dating in the workplace, but we all know that it happens. If you happen to find love at work, the best thing to do is to keep the relationship low-key until the two of you decide that it is moving toward a more permanent relationship. In the meantime, make sure that you don't address your partner by any terms or expressions that are anything other than professional, and never, ever display any signs of public affection.

Once the relationship is solidified and you think he might be a keeper, you can acknowledge the relationship to a few close friends and even attend social events together. Before you do any of this, it's best that the two of you are moving toward marriage.

Workplace Dress Code

To determine the dress code at your current job, check with your colleagues, human resources department, or even your manager to ask exactly what is acceptable. It's always better to ask and be clear rather than make a major faux pas.

Many workplaces now designate casual dress days. Casual-day attire is open to interpretation depending on a company's culture. At some companies, casual might mean jeans and a T-shirt, while at other jobs casual means that the men are not required to wear a suit jacket.

Your best bet is to dress a bit more formally than you normally would for your first few days at work (perhaps the type of outfits you might wear to an interview) and keep an eye out to see what other employees wear, then follow suit.

Sexual Harassment in the Workplace

In the past, sexual harassment almost exclusively referred to a male harassing a woman. As more women move up the corporate ladder, it has become a two-way street. In today's workplace, it is more important than ever to keep your behavior completely professional. Keep in mind that what you may consider an innocent comment can be perceived by others as anything but professional. To ensure that your behavior is not misconstrued as inappropriate, avoid making comments about your employees' or coworkers' appearance and personal lives. Also, it is very important to avoid playing favorites in the office. Any favoritism (perceived or valid) can cause others in the office to suspect that preferential treatment is due to a sexual relationship or attraction.

At the same time, it is important to know when other people's behavior toward you crosses the line. If someone says something to you in the workplace that makes you uncomfortable, you should tell the person immediately rather than ignoring it and hoping that it doesn't happen again. You can say something really simple like, "Your compliments (or behavior, or questions) make me uncomfortable and I wish you would stop." This should be enough to deflect any unwanted attention. If the person persists, you should contact your human resources department and ask for assistance. In the past, employers would often turn the other cheek, especially if the harasser was higher up in the company. However, this attitude of ignoring the problem has changed drastically, and more companies are taking the allegations seriously.

Searching for a New Job

Some of the most important issues regarding etiquette in the workplace arise in the process of looking for alternative employment, especially if your current employer is not aware that you are looking for a new gig. The following suggestions will help to ensure that you conduct yourself professionally and wisely while looking for a new job.

Where to Look

You loved your job and your company when you started working. Now, you've decided it's time to leave. Regardless of the reason, job searches can take a while, so while you're casting your net, remember to keep information about your job search limited to very close friends and contacts who you know might be able to provide job leads. You want your boss to find out about your job search when you submit your resignation—and not one minute earlier. As the saying goes, "It's easier to find a job when you already have one," so keep your search discreet.

A good place to start your job search is through any networking group that you may belong to. These are organizations that you identify with based on your career choice, such as the Society of Female Engineers, the Public Relations Society of America, or the National Black MBA association. Not only are these organizations committed to advancing the industry, but they also are one of the best sources for job openings. Also consider any online networking groups, such as LinkedIn. However, be aware that current coworkers or employers may also be in this network.

Another option is to attend career fairs and establish contacts for new job possibilities. For instance, if you know of former coworkers who have moved on to better positions, contact them and inquire if there are any possibilities with their new employer. Whenever you receive a lead or make contact with someone through your networking, always send a letter thanking the person for his or her time and assistance.

Popular websites such as Careerbuilder.com and Monster.com post jobs in all industries across the country. If you're interested in relocating, these sites make it easy to search for jobs in a new city or state. They also post advice on interviewing, networking, and writing follow-up letters.

When you get a positive job lead, ask the employer to contact you on your cell phone or after work hours at your home. Refrain from conducting phone interviews in your office or cubicle during company hours.

Resume

Your resume is usually the first introduction to a potential employer. Since you're often competing with dozens (sometime hundreds) of other hopeful job candidates, that piece of paper has to speak loudly and clearly on your behalf. A resume should always be:

- **Brief but informative.** Two pages is the maximum length but one page is better.
- **Honest.** Yes, you may be applying for a manager's position. If you haven't had that type of experience, don't say that you do. Always tell the truth on your resume.

∾ **Easy to read and understand.** Use off-white or white paper and use 10- or 12-point type. Do not type your resume on neon-colored paper or put graphics and borders on your paper.

Keep your list of references handy and updated. As you apply for different jobs, always contact your references to let them know that you are listing them as a referral. If someone isn't happy about being used as a reference, you need to know so that you won't submit his or her name.

Job interview

If your resume does the job, you'll be called in for an interview. When preparing for an interview, you should always review whatever information you can locate on the company. Look up articles on the Internet and review annual reports so that you are informed about the mission of the company, new products, or even management decisions.

Dress appropriately and wear a conservative suit. If you're applying for a job with a more creative dress code, you don't have to be as conservative, but you should still wear a suit. Be sure to bring an extra resume to the interview. You can also bring any documents that detail your areas of expertise or describe relevant projects you've worked on. Make sure that you carry all papers in a professional portfolio or briefcase.

Be sure to arrive at the interview fifteen minutes early so that you can find a parking spot, locate the site of the interview, take a few minutes to compose yourself, and review your research one last time. During the interview, be sure to speak clearly and confidently, and ask questions at the end of the interview. Asking questions shows that you have researched the company and can clear up questions you might have about the direction of the company, growth opportunities, and even corporate structure. The answers to your questions could help you decide if this is a company where you want to work. After the interview, be sure to send a thank-you note that emphasizes your skills and your desire to work for the new company. If you are interviewed by more than one person, send a separate follow-up note to everyone who interviewed you.

Dear Mr. Murphy,

It was a pleasure meeting with you earlier this week to discuss the senior manager position with your company. I would like to thank you for your time and confirm my strong interest in the position and your company.

As we discussed, I feel that my education and background in marketing as well as brand building and advertising will prove to be an asset to your company. Additionally, I am a hard worker, creative, and a loyal employee. I am confident that I can make a valuable contribution to your company and the marketing department.

I look forward to hearing from you.

Sincerely,
Christopher Kranz

Resigning

As thrilled as you may be to resign from your current job, your final meeting with your boss is not the time to get any feelings of ill will off your chest. Even upon your exit, you don't want to burn any bridges.

You should offer a resignation letter to your boss as well to neatly tie up all loose ends. The letter should be brief and include the date your resignation is effective, your last day at work, and of course a brief line about how you really enjoyed working for that company. You never know what the future holds. You might want to return to your company at some point in the future or you might end up working under your same boss again. Always be courteous even on your way out the door. A sample letter is below:

Dear Sarah O'Brien,

Please accept this letter as my official letter of resignation from Benchmark Media, effective on Friday, March 27, 2008. As I've stated to you many times over the years, I have thoroughly enjoyed the work environment and professional atmosphere at Benchmark. Your management, guidance, direction, and support have been the source of great personal and career satisfaction for me.

The experience and knowledge gained during my employment at Benchmark has provided significant career growth for which I shall always be appreciative.

Sincerely,
Jennifer R. Fox

It is important to conduct yourself with class and sensitivity when moving on from a job. Be mindful of coworker's feelings (as well as the extra tasks they may have to take on in your absence) when leaving a job. Regardless of how you feel about leaving, it will serve you to be remembered as a thoughtful and considerate coworker rather than someone who shrugged off duties and expressed glee over jumping ship.

Losing A Job

In today's world of downsizing and mergers, the possibility of losing a job looms closer to everyone. If this happens to you, it's time to put on your game face and keep coming to the office until your last day. Tie up loose ends and turn over work that needs to be completed to your peers or your manager. Take the time to meet with your human resources manager to discuss your benefits, the length of time you will be paid, any unused vacation days, and possible opportunities within the company that are outside of your department. Be sure to ask about the company's outplacement services as well. Often, the company will offer job search tools for those who are departing the company. Once your last day at work is completed, you should methodically write down a list of people that can possibly help you find a job and start utilizing your contacts.

Although the daily grind of the job can be rewarding or sometimes wear you down, you should still mind your manners from 9 to 5. As the saying goes, you should be careful on your way up the ladder because you never know who you will see on your way down. You want to be remembered for your drive, persistence, and, yes, even your manners.

technology and etiquette

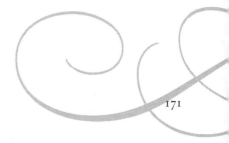

With my boss, Deanna, still out of the office on maternity leave, I am now the lucky recipient of approximately twenty e-mails a day from her. I thought her leave would give me space to breathe, but it's only made my job that much harder.

This morning, after checking and responding to most of my work e-mails, I log in to my personal e-mail account. These e-mails are a welcome reprieve. It's nice to be able to check in with friends and family when I'm so buried at the office. This morning, I open a message that extols the joy of motherhood. It has such a warm slant that I forward it to Deanna and a few other moms that I know.

"I saw this e-mail and thought of you!" I include at the top of the forward, and click send.

Deanna must be in a good mood this morning because she immediately writes back to thank me for thinking of her. Seeing an influx of work e-mails pop up on my screen, I forget all about the forward and get back to work.

Later that afternoon, my phone rings. It's Deanna sounding perturbed, which is nothing unusual.

"Meagan, why did you give my e-mail address to your friend Joy?" she asks.

"I didn't give your address to Joy, Deanna. I . . ."

"Well, you do know a Joy, don't you?"

Before I could respond, she continues, "She invited me to her facial party and specifically says that she is a friend of yours. So, obviously, she got the address from you. Please tell her to take me off her distribution list." And with that, she hung up.

I was furious as I logged into my e-mail account to find an invite from my friend Joy—with Deanna's name on the invite list.

Clicking back to the forward I sent out that morning, I realize that I did not "bcc" the e-mail, but instead included the addresses in the "to" section. I rarely do that and I don't know how or why I forgot this time—especially since I included Deanna on the e-mail. ❧

T echnology is taking over our lives—with our permission, of course. What would you do if you lost your cell phone? Your life wouldn't be the same until your phone is safely tucked in your purse again. And then there's your computer. Snail mail, or mail that comes to your house or place of business in an envelope, is fading to black. We pay our bills online, look up entertainment options, talk to friends, view our pay stubs, and stay in touch with people via e-mail.

E-mail makes it easy to drop someone a line and say "How are you," or "I read about your engagement in the paper," or even "Hi, I haven't spoken to you in a while. I heard about a job at Company X and I thought you might be interested." Even though staying in touch is easier and done with the click of a button, there are still certain guidelines that those sending and receiving e-mail should follow.

anissa says ...

Stay reserved in e-mails at work. Even when you're very familiar with the colleague you are corresponding with, always remain professional. Do not use all caps, smiley faces, or unnecessary exclamation points.

The Basic Netiquette of E-mails

E-mail is quickly becoming the preferred mode of communication because of its speed and efficiency and the ability to contact several people simultaneously. However, with all of the advantages and perks to e-mail, users should still proceed with caution, especially when e-mailing from the workplace.

Privacy

In almost all cases, all e-mails sent from your business computer belong to your employer. When using your business e-mail address, the user must realize that an employer can read all e-mails and there is no such entity as privacy. Additionally, if you log in to your personal e-mail address from your work computer, these messages most often fall under your company's Internet policy and may be read.

Anything that is private should not be sent via e-mail when other options are available. If you want to send a personal e-mail, wait until you have access to a computer outside of the workplace. If the information is really private, consider making a phone call instead of using e-mail.

meagan says ...

If you do send a message erroneously, either to the wrong person or the e-mail contains information about a person who also received it, you should take responsibility and apologize to anyone involved.

When it comes to e-mails regarding work, there are also topics that are better discussed in person or on the phone. Any type of serious information should not be sent via e-mail. Depending on your office culture, this could include criticism of a job performance, salary information, downsizing notices, terminations, business plans, and letters of resignation.

Not only is it inappropriate to notify someone of a serious mater over e-mail, but there is also the possibility that you could send the information to an incorrect e-mail address, or that your technology department could intercept your e-mail.

technology and etiquette

Choosing an E-mail Address

Usually, your work address will be designated for you and users must follow certain guidelines. When selecting a user name for your personal account, be sure to choose a name that isn't offensive to others or that may reflect negatively on your job if your boss was to learn of the name.

If you have a personal e-mail address that you created when you were younger, you may want to consider updating it to reflect your maturity. There may come a time when you would like to share your e-mail address for the purpose of finding a new job or include your personal e-mail address on your resume. It is best to have an e-mail address that includes some iteration of your first and last name (e.g., *MeaganLSmith@Emailname.com*), or perhaps your industry (*PersonalChef27@Emailname.com*) rather than your love for your favorite band or your middle school nickname.

If you decide to change your e-mail address, send an e-mail to all of your e-mail contacts to let them know. Again, make sure that the new e-mail address is a name that won't embarrass you and one that you can put on your resume.

Crossing Your Ts and Dotting Your Is

When writing e-mails, especially of the professional nature, keep in mind that you should use proper punctuation, spelling, and grammar.

cal says ...

You will probably have a list of friends whom you e-mail during the day. Keep in mind the addresses you are using and respect your friends' request that e-mails be limited only to their personal mailbox, if necessary.

Use all uppercase letters only when you want to stress a point: "Hi Casey. I really LOVED the sweater your mother made me. I can't wait to see you because I'll be wearing it."

Poor grammar or typos signal laziness and also makes e-mails difficult to understand. Using proper grammar, punctuation, and spelling makes communication easier and more effective.

Always include a distinct topic in the subject line so that the e-mail message recipient knows what the contents of the e-mail contain. E-mails should also, especially in a professional setting, include a salutation, similar to a letter. Hello, Hi, or even Good Morning or Good Afternoon are all appropriate openings. You can close an e-mail by using, Thank you, or Sincerely, before hitting the send button.

Just because e-mails are read on screen does not mean that you should lower your professionalism.

The Permanence of E-mails

Some people tie letters together with a fancy ribbon and read them over and over again, savoring the memories and smiling at the words. Well, e-mails are like a bundle of letters too—except they don't fade with time. E-mails can be stored forever, so use caution when sending e-mails. Even hitting the delete button does not permanently erase all e-mails. Words that you can write can come back to haunt you, although the hope is that you don't get into any situation where your e-mails are used against you.

The Privacy of E-mails (or Lack Thereof)

Sometimes your friends send jokes or forward e-mails that command that you send the e-mail to ten people or else you'll have seven years of bad luck or some other nonsense. Some may enjoy getting humorous or touching e-mails and will continue the chain. Most people actually don't like forwarded e-mails, and when that is the case, they should let the sender know that they would like to be removed from the sender's list. Due to the volume of e-mails that most people get every day, the basic rule is not to send e-mail forwards (especially if the recipient will get seven years of bad luck if she doesn't forward the e-mail to twenty-five people). If the message contains an inspirational message and you really want to share it, be sure to send it to a few select friends, rather than everyone in your address book.

If you are the sender, there are a few netiquette steps you can take to protect your recipients' e-mail privacy so that they don't start receiving erroneous e-mails from strangers.

First, if forwarding an e-mail, be sure to erase all e-mail addresses in the body of the e-mail. Second, use the bcc (blind carbon copy) line when addressing an e-mail to a large group of people, especially if some are colleagues and others are not. The last thing you want to happen is for

meagan says ...

When you receive an e-mail that is sent to several e-mail recipients, be careful when forming a response. If the e-mail is one that you should answer, only respond to the sender of the e-mail. Do not hit "Reply All" unless absolutely necessary.

your distant friend to get your manager's e-mail address from an e-mail you sent and e-mail her and ask for a job.

Confidential Information

There is always the possibility that you might send an e-mail to the wrong Theresa or Joe in your address book. The mistake is easy to make when you type in the first few letters of a name and your address book brings up four to five options. Because of this, you should always take extreme caution when sending personal or confidential information via e-mail. The best route is never to send private information over e-mail. But if necessary, be very careful.

Connecting Strangers via E-mail

Just like a home or office telephone number or even a cell phone number, you should never give out a person's e-mail address without first asking permission. If the person agrees that it is okay to forward this information, you can send an e-mail to both parties and make a virtual introduction.

Social Networking

It seems like everyone is on Facebook, Myspace, LinkedIn, or another social networking site. Take your pick and inevitably someone will ask if you have a page on one of these sites. Some use the sites to meet people and add "friends," while others advertise their wares to drum up business. Although meeting a long lost friend on MySpace is a wonderful thing, you should still update your personal site with care. Sure, it's perfectly all right to list your hobbies and basic information about yourself. You do, however, want to stay away from any subject that might be offensive to your current employer or a new employer. In the information age, jobs now review your resume as well as your Internet presence. Needless to say, if your page says that you hate your boss or that you think the CEO of your company is going in the wrong direction, you could be fired from your job. Also, those statements could certainly prevent another company from hiring you. Last, your comments and opinions on other people's sites are stored in virtual memory. So, be careful about what you post, even if it's not on your page.

Online Dating

We've all seen the commercials that tout the success of couples who met online, dated, and now are totally head-over-heels in love and, in some cases, married. Who wouldn't want that? If they can find love via a dating

Technology makes keeping in touch easier, but being polite and considerate is still necessary.

site, why can't you? Online dating is very popular now and is an easy way to meet people who also are looking for companionship. Popular sites such as Match.com and eHarmony even have a screening process to increase the odds of your compatibility with select others on the site.

As with all dating, the first rule of thumb with online dating, which is akin to blind dating until you meet, is to proceed with caution.

Once you've had a few online conversations with the person and you decide that you want to meet face-to-face, always meet in a public place and plan to keep the first date short. If you decide to proceed after your initial date, then wait a few more dates to allow the date to pick you up from your house or even invite him to your home at all.

If want to end a relationship or stop seeing someone you met online, the same rules apply as to any other relationship: always be straightforward with how you feel, while being mindful of his feelings.

Cell Phone Etiquette

It seems like everyone lives with their cell phone attached to them. Here are guidelines so that you don't commit a faux pas when chatting on your cell.

- ∾ Don't hold conversations at the dining table. If you receive a call that you must answer, leave the table and go to a secluded spot.
- ∾ When entering a place of worship, concert hall, theater, or a restaurant, turn off the ringer so that others will not be disturbed.

- Avoid talking on the phone, even with an earpiece, when you are in public places including the shopping mall, grocery store, or at a local park. If you must use the phone, keep your voice low and conversation quiet and quick.

Text Messages

Text messages, just like e-mails, have ruined reputations and careers. Texting is fun, quick, and sometimes necessary. Although most cell phone plans do not permanently save text messages, there are some companies that do store the messages. Make sure you do not send a message that will come back to haunt you. And just like e-mails, be sure you're sending the text to the right recipient before your message intended for your friend goes to your boss.

When you are in the company of others, limit your texting to that which is absolutely necessary. If you are dining and receive an urgent text message, excuse yourself and go to a separate area where you are free to communicate. And never, ever text while driving.

Camera Phones

It can be fun to snap a picture on your camera phone when you're out at happy hour or to capture your nephew's first at-bat at his Little League game and send it on to your sister who couldn't be there. In some settings however, camera phones should not be used. Concerts, courtrooms, and museums are a few places that ban the use of any type of picture taking.

Likewise, you should not use your camera phone to take photos of anyone without their consent. You will run the risk of appearing rude.

BlackBerry Devices

The BlackBerry has become a ubiquitous necessity among business professionals. Because of its omnipresence, the BlackBerry has been nicknamed the "crackberry." Here are some general guidelines so you're not labeled as an addict.

In general, the rules are the same for the BlackBerry as for the cell phone. The phone should be turned on silent during a meeting, and if one must take a call or respond to an e-mail, step outside of the meeting to do so. Only when you are waiting for important information should you check your e-mails during a meeting. And, if that's the case, you should alert the manager in the meeting that you might have to duck out to accept a call or review an e-mail. Turn your BlackBerry down when dining with friends or colleagues and when entering meetings or places of worship.

Although technology is ever present in all aspects of our lives and we are often communicating with someone that we can't see, common sense is still necessary. Don't use the phone when you are face-to-face with others; respect others' time and don't bombard friends with silly e-mails; and even when love enters the air, proceed with caution. Technology makes keeping in touch easier, but being polite and considerate is still necessary.

CHAPTER 12

the perfect host, the perfect guest

Saturday morning I was still chilling out in my PJs catching up on my DVR. In the middle of my shows, I paused the TV to answer my phone.

Before I can even finish saying, "Hello," Anissa jumps right in.

"I can't take another minute," says Anissa. "Melissa is *killing* me."

Melissa is a friend of ours from college. She and Anissa had stayed in touch sporadically, and when Melissa called and said she would be in town for a conference, Anissa extended her home for the weekend. And now, she was paying for it. I always knew Melissa was quirky, but Anissa always liked her. Now, her patience was wearing thin.

"What is she doing?" I ask. "I thought you guys were getting along. You hung out together last night, right?"

"Yeah and that was cool, but when we got home, she just started taking me for granted." Anissa went on to say that when she and Melissa returned to the house, Melissa insisted on switching rooms with Anissa because the TV in the guest room was too small. Being a generous host, Anissa agreed to switch rooms with Melissa just to keep the peace.

"I think that was a bit much to ask to switch beds," fumes Anissa. "I mean, what would she have done if I was married? Asked my husband and me to sleep in the guest room?"

Anissa continued to tell me that earlier that morning, Melissa got out of the bed at 6 A.M., crashed around the kitchen making herself breakfast, and then left in Anissa's car before she could get out of bed.

"Oh my goodness, she actually drove off in your car?" I asked. Anissa had my full attention at that point because that was really crossing the line. "Well, you only have one more day with her," I said, trying to be supportive, "but when she returns, you should definitely lay down some ground rules and hide your car keys."

Needless to say, Anissa was very, very upset. When we hung up the phone, I wasn't sure if Melissa should ever step across Anissa's threshold again. Not even to return the car keys. ❧

As the saying goes, houseguests are like fish—after three days, they both stink. Visiting relatives and friends is usually a great time. There's nothing like catching up on old times, with the people you love. However, when your visit entails a stay at someone's house, there are guidelines you should adhere to—especially if you want to be invited back.

Be the Perfect Guest

When staying at someone's home, whether overnight or for a longer visit, you have certain obligations to your host. This section will outline most of them to ensure that you don't become that houseguest from hell.

A GUEST'S *Obligations* TO HER HOST

Share your travel plans early: Contact your host prior to finalizing travel plans to be sure there are no conflicts with the host's schedule. Confirm your arrival and departure time and also advise if you will need a ride or assistance. Make sure that you don't stay too long. You should depart at the time you originally planned and not extend your stay—unless it's due to unforeseen circumstances.

Leave your pets at home: Don't ask to bring your pet unless you are very close friends with your host. Even then, if your pet is unruly, not accustomed to children (if the host has kids), and rough on furniture and rugs, check Ranger into a doggy hotel.

A GUEST'S *Obligations* TO HER HOST

Bring your personal toiletries: Pack your own shampoo, toothpaste, soap, and other toiletries rather than relying on your host for these items. If you don't have use of a private bathroom, keep your toiletries in a case rather than spread out over the shared bathroom.

Prepare your children for the visit: If you are traveling with children, make sure that you pack their favorite snacks since your host might not have these items. Also, talk to your host to determine what areas in the house are okay for snacking and abide by those rules.

Chip in with the chores: Don't wait for your host to ask for your help. Nor should your offer to help be open-ended, "Let me know if I can help with anything." Make a specific offer such as "Let me wash the dishes or clean the kitchen." Unless your host responds with a firm "no thanks" to your offer, you should do what you can to keep the home clean and neat.

Be neat: In addition to helping to straighten and clean common areas, you should also clean up the bathroom after using it, including washing out the sink and putting away any toiletries. Keep the guest room neat and make up the bed every day. If sharing a bathroom with your host or other guests, don't hog the bathroom by taking a leisurely bath or use up all the hot water by taking a long shower. If you are sleeping in a common area, remove your sheets everyday and ask where you should store the linens.

A GUEST'S *Obligations* TO HER HOST

Participate in planned activities: If your host has planned a day of camping and you're not really the outdoorsy type, you should still go along and try to enjoy yourself. If on the other hand your host is chilling out at home for the day, go with the flow as well.

Give your host time to relax: You should not expect your host to entertain you every waking hour. If your host is relaxing, figure out an activity that you can do on your own time, like going shopping, visiting a museum, or reading a book. If you decide to venture out, discuss your plans with your host so that she can make use of her time alone as well. Your independence gives the host time to take care of personal business.

Don't use the phone unless necessary: This is becoming less of an issue as most of us have cell phones. Be sure to keep the ringer off so that it doesn't disturb others. If you can't get cell service where you are and need to use your host's phone, keep conversations brief.

Treat your host: Take your host to dinner during your stay. Make sure you let her know the date and time so that she can make appropriate plans. Also, if you're out shopping with your host, pick up the tab for small expenses such as toiletries and household items.

Discuss additional plans in advance with your host: If you want to attend the theater or even visit other friends during your visit, you should discuss your plans with your host in advance and ask the best time to coordinate those activities. Do not make plans or accept plans for you or your host without first asking your host.

A GUEST'S *Obligations* TO HER HOST

Follow the schedule of your host: Typically, your host determines the time to go to bed and what time to get out of bed. Try to adhere to that schedule. Keep your voice down in the evening and keep the television low, especially late at night or early morning.

Do not smoke inside: Unless your host is a smoker and invites you to light up, do not make the assumption that it's all right to smoke indoors. If you must have a cigarette, ask your host where you can smoke outdoors and be sure to gather your cigarette butts.

Straighten up before you leave: Before you leave, remove your sheets from the bed, fold them, and place them at the end of the bed. Also, ask your hostess what you should do with your used towels.

Bring a small hostess gift. When staying in someone's home, it's always a nice and much appreciated gesture to bring your host or hostess a gift. Suggestions for appropriate guests follow in the next section.

Send a thank-you: In addition to thanking your host in person when you say goodbye, send a thank-you card to your host. The thank-you note should be sent within a few days after you return. If you and your spouse both stayed overnight, only one of you needs to write the letter. Only the person writing the letter signs his or her name. If your children were also guests, include that the children had a good time as well. You also can compliment the home, the view, and any specific activities that you enjoyed. A sample thank-you note is on the following page.

A GUEST'S *Obligations* TO HER HOST

> *Dear Claire,*
>
> *You and Grant showed us a great time at your beach house this past week-end. Victoria and Lucas especially enjoyed the fishing trip. Cooking our catch over the open fire was a special experience and made the food taste even better. Adam and I look forward to returning the favor at our home and spending the weekend together again soon. Thank you all so much.*
>
> *Sincerely,*
> *Roberta*

Hostess Gifts

Thank-you gifts are required whenever you have spent time as a guest in someone's home. Although gifts don't have to be expensive, you should consider how much your guests entertained you and also compare the stay at your friend's house to the cost of a hotel stay. You can bring the gift with you and present it when you arrive or before you leave, but you still have to send a thank-you note after departing.

Bringing a gift for the hostess is a gracious gesture. However, some events, like a cocktail party or an open house, don't require a gift. But when attending a dinner party or staying overnight at your host's home, then you should give your host a small gift to show your appreciation.

Hostess gifts should not require any extra attention by the host, especially if presented prior to a party. If your host is managing the ins and outs of a party, she doesn't need to find a vase for flowers or feel pressure to serve the wine you brought. Gifts of food and drink are acceptable if you make it clear that the gift should be enjoyed at a later date. If you do bring flowers for an event, they should be in a vase. If you want to send cut flowers, have them delivered the day before or after the event.

When making your selection, gifts to consider could be based on your host's favorite color or one of her hobbies. The gift doesn't have to be expensive; thoughtful presents work just as well. Here are some ideas for great hostess gifts:

- ‿ A variety of teas combined with a small teapot and sugar is a good gift for the tea lover.
- ‿ A basket filled with local treats from the gift giver's hometown, or if the recipient has recently relocated, treats that reflect her hometown.
- ‿ A basket of gourmet cheese and crackers on an attractive cheese platter, made from slate or stone, is a tasty treat.
- ‿ A music CD that reflects the preferences of the host is a good gift for the music lover or the host who loves to entertain. You can also create a party mix on your own.
- ‿ A collection of specialty seasonings is a welcome and useful gift for someone who enjoys cooking.
- ‿ Picture frames are nice, affordable gifts. You can even insert a picture of you and the hostess that depicts a good time the two of you had together.

- A set of candles can be used to add ambience at the host's next party or when she decides to unwind after her guests have left.
- Fragrant hand soaps and lotions help the hostess keep her hands smooth and fragrant.
- A recipe journal for the experimental cook will provide her with an orderly way to sort and store her recipes.
- Gourmet olive oil adds a kick to the cook's recipes and is perfect for the hostess who doesn't drink wine.
- An assortment of cocktail mixers will help the host get a head start on planning her next party.
- If you like to bake and the hostess doesn't, a basket full of your favorite homemade cookie dough and baking mixes will be appreciated.
- A new cookbook, especially a signed one, from the host's favorite chef may help inspire her next menu.
- A box of stationery or pretty note cards is a gift that your host can use for thank-you cards.
- An elegant centerpiece for your host's table, especially at holiday time, will make a statement for the host as well as any guests that visit.
- Wine glass charms are an easy way for guests to identify their glass. Your host will appreciate the charms, the use of multiple glasses will decrease, and other guests also will like the charms.
- Chocolate desserts for the hostess to enjoy are sure to be a hit for the chocolate lover.

- ～ Hand-painted cocktail or martini glasses will add pizzazz for the hostess who likes to entertain and shake up drinks.
- ～ Personalized beer mugs and pints will be a delight and probably become one the host's favorite drinking glasses.
- ～ Create a basket of breakfast treats for the hostess and her family to enjoy.
- ～ For the game lover, a new edition of a classic board game, or a newer game she has not yet tried, is a fun gift.

Regardless of the gift, try to give a present that reflects the hostess and her likes. And remember that it's not necessary for the host to send the guest a thank-you card.

Now that you know how to be a perfect houseguest, here are some tips to ensure that you are an equally gracious host.

Preparing for the Guest

It takes time and effort to prepare for an overnight guest. Make your guests feel at home by preparing the guest room, cleaning, and providing good food, conversation, and even entertainment. When you have a visitor at your home, it is a great time for you, your boyfriend, husband, or family to break your regular routine and plan something fun and exciting for your guest. Certainly, your guests don't want to stay a few days with you and the highlight of the weekend is watching television.

Your plan for your guest doesn't have to include wild excursions, but it could consist of planning a small cocktail party and introducing her to your friends, checking out the new exhibit at a local museum, or venturing out to try a new restaurant.

You should try to have something planned, especially when the guest will be there for a few days or the weekend. If your guests are staying longer than a few days, you are not obligated to drop your schedule and entertain them everyday, but taking your guests out on a few of the days is considered good manners.

Prepping the Guest Room

Getting the guest room prepared and cozy lets your guest know that you have been excited and awaiting her arrival. A few things you can do to make the room cozy are to place fresh flowers, the newspapers of the day and current magazines, and even a carafe of water and drinking glasses in the guest room or the room where your guest is sleeping. Leaving chocolates on the pillow also is a nice touch and will welcome your guest while providing a tasty treat.

Although your guests will probably bring their own toiletries, a good host will still stock the powder room with toothpaste, deodorant, lotions, and soaps, just in case your guest forgets a few items. Hanging a clean bathrobe in the closet also is a nice touch. You should also provide guest towels in the powder room.

The following is a checklist for the days leading up to your guest's arrival.

OVERNIGHT GUEST PREPARATION LIST

- One Week Before
  - Contact your guest and confirm arrival time.
  - Select a room or designate a sleeping area for the guest and clear out closet space.
  - Select guest sheets and towels and make bed if the guest will have the luxury of sleeping in a guest room.
  - Plan your menus.
  - Review the local papers for upcoming activities to have ideas for a proposed agenda.
- One Day Before
  - Clean the bedroom and powder room.
  - Leave guest towels in the powder room.
  - Complete your grocery shopping, including any stops to the liquor store if you would like to stock your bar.
- Day of Arrival
  - Place chocolates on the pillow and place flowers, books, and magazines by the bed

GUEST BEDROOM (OR SLEEPING AREA) NECESSITIES

- Fresh sheets for the bed
- Bedside reading lamp
- Closet, with hangers, and drawer space for the guest's clothes
- Clock with alarm

- ❧ Nightlight
- ❧ Books and magazines
- ❧ Extra pillows and an extra blanket at the foot of the bed
- ❧ Slippers and a robe

GUEST POWDER ROOM NECESSITIES

- ❧ Fresh, unused soap
- ❧ New roll of toilet paper
- ❧ Bath mat
- ❧ Matching hand, face, and bath towels
- ❧ New toothbrush and new package of toothpaste
- ❧ Shampoo and conditioner
- ❧ Lotion
- ❧ Scented candles and air freshener
- ❧ Mouthwash and dental floss
- ❧ Cotton balls and swabs
- ❧ Aspirin
- ❧ Band-aids

Arrival of the Guest

When your guests arrive, try to be at your home to greet them and, if necessary, give them a tour of the home or room where they will stay. If for some reason you can't be at the home, then you should let them know in advance and leave a welcome note that clearly lays out any house particulars including where the guest room and bathroom are located, if there is a separate one for the guests' use, food in the refrigerator, and how to lock or unlock the doors.

If you are very organized and like everything in an orderly fashion, you can even create an itinerary of all the activities you have planned for your guest and leave it out for him or her to look over. This is not necessary, but it is thoughtful to offer some suggestions.

You should, however, discuss an agenda, if you have one, or ask your guests what they would like to do, and plan an agenda together.

The Not-So-Good Guest

Every once in a while, our wonderful friend turns into a not so wonderful guest. Sometimes the friend becomes tipsy, belligerent, or offensive to other guests. When you can tell that an awkward situation is brewing, you should do your best to circumvent the situation or prevent it from escalating.

When a guest cracks an offensive joke, you should step in and interrupt before the punch line is delivered. You can change the subject by asking a question that will take the conversation in a totally different direction. For instance, asking the guest to tell everyone about a recent trip to Greece should suffice. Or, the host can ask the guest to help with something that will remove him or her from the room.

Different tactics are needed for overnight guests who have started to wear out their welcome. First, before they arrive, ask what their plans are for the visit. This includes arrival time and the day of departure. If either the arrival or departure time is not convenient for you, you should advise the guest of this before they solidify their plans.

If your guest is still at your home a few days after he said he would leave, the time has come to be firm. You can drop a hint and ask indirectly when the guest plans to leave, or what happened to his previous travel plans. If that doesn't work, and sometimes it won't, you will have to ask the guest to leave. Be polite, but firm. You can say something like, "I thought you were leaving last Wednesday. You've been here an extra four days, and while I've really enjoyed you, I would like to get my house back to normal. I need you to make plans to leave tomorrow morning." Otherwise, you can get ready to add another person to your household.

CHAPTER 13

tact during
sad times

Like most new parents, Cal and Jimmy have been pretty busy taking care of Chase. Even though they're occupied with the baby, they still manage to find time to hang out with us every once in a while.

The last few times Anissa and I met, Cal arrived very late because she had started checking in on her elderly neighbor next door. Every day, she brought dinner to Mrs. Tullie. Even if she and Jimmy didn't cook for themselves, Cal would take her something to eat. As a result of seeing her so often, Chase absolutely loved her and was too young to realize that she was very sick and usually in the bed when they visited.

Cal had told us that Mrs. Tullie didn't have any local family, but her daughter, who lived in Texas, had been in and out of town every few weeks. Mrs. Tullie was widowed and had retired as a bank vice president fifteen years ago. Cal, being the concerned and compassionate person that she always is, committed her Saturday mornings to straightening up Mrs. Tullie's home and running any errands she might need.

One Saturday, Anissa and I were waiting for Cal to arrive for lunch at our favorite restaurant. Neither of us saw Cal walk in, and when she approached us we were still in deep conversation. Her face was red, her eyes were swollen, and she was sniffling. Anissa stopped in midsentence and grabbed her in a bear hug.

"Cal, what's wrong?" asked Anissa.

Then Cal really broke down. She started crying so hard that people in the lobby stopped and stared.

"Mrs. Tullie died last night," she choked out.

Anissa and I both looked at her sympathetically. We knew that Cal, Jimmy, and Chase had grown very attached to her.

"Last night she called and said she wasn't feeling well, so Jimmy and I took her to the hospital," said Cal. "She saw the doctor who said she was a little dehydrated but seemed fine. Jimmy and I left her there around 11 o'clock and came home. The doctor called us this morning to relay the news." Cal dabbed at her eyes and continued. "Jimmy and I would really like to help out with the services, but since we barely know her family, we'd probably just get in the way."

At this point, we guided Cal out of the restaurant since none of us felt like eating at this point. We went back to Cal's house to stay with her, and Jimmy made us lunch. After we ate, Anissa and I promised to be there for Cal at the funeral and for anything else she needed. ❧

W hen someone dies, often we are at a loss of words and simply don't know what to say or do. That could be because there is no standard for grieving nor any segue to make death and dying a subject that we are comfortable discussing and encountering.

Regardless of the grieving process, the family and loved ones of the deceased still needs love and support. This chapter will give you the basic information you need to be a supportive friend or family member during this difficult time.

Lending a Helping Hand to the Family

When someone you are close to loses a family member, you can start helping them out even before the actual funeral takes place. Contact the family and offer your condolences, as well as to help out in any way.

The ways that you can help people who are grieving a loss are varied. Whenever there is a death, families usually have several guests and visitors to their home before the wake, funeral, or memorial services. Food is always welcome, and you can help out by bringing a favorite dish of the family or even one that is your specialty. You can bring foods over the first few days and even weeks and months afterward when you continue to check on the family (especially if a mother or father has been left to raise children on their own, or an elderly widow or widower is living alone). Grief has many stages and often is a very long process. Being supportive before and after the funeral is helpful to the family.

Chipping in with answering the phone, making arrangements, and even cleaning up will all be welcomed by the family members. If you are a close friend, don't wait to be asked to help—pitch in when and where you can. If in doubt about where the family needs assistance, consider the following:

- ❧ Help entertain and talk with visitors who stop by.
- ❧ Prepare plates and drinks for visitors and clean up after them.
- ❧ Babysit young children or keep them occupied.
- ❧ Keep track of floral arrangements and gift baskets so that the family can send thank-you notes.
- ❧ Answer the telephone and take messages for the family as well as provide information about the family if needed.

Notifying Family and Others

When a family member dies, a relative will often make calls to other family and friends to alert them of the news. Often, the family is very distraught, and as a close friend of the family, it is a very nice gesture to offer to make the calls on their behalf. The family is usually glad to have help when contacting others, so feel free to volunteer your time to make the calls. If you are notifying people of the death, you should also have an idea of when and where the services might take place, especially if the deceased has a church home. You also can give your contact information and advise friends to call the family of the deceased or you to firm up details about the services.

Helping to Make Arrangements

If you are helping out the family to make funeral arrangements, it is important that you inquire about religious tradition. Depending on the family's faith, the funeral proceedings may be very particular.

In the Jewish tradition, the body should be buried as soon as possible after the death, often the next day. Jewish law mandates that the body is protected from desecration, willful or not, until burial. Two of the main requirements are the showing of proper respect for the body of the deceased and the ritual cleansing of the body and dressing for burial.

Traditionally, Christians bury the body as soon as possible, usually within a week, but allow time for out-of-town relatives to arrive so they can attend the funeral.

Hindu traditions involve cremation to dispose of the body. Cremation practices became popular due to the notion that the soul cannot enter a new body until its former one has completely disappeared.

Islamic funerals follow specific rites and rituals for burying the dead and are performed as soon as possible. The burial consists of placing the body in a grave and positioning the deceased's head toward Mecca.

At the Wake or Funeral

Get to the wake or funeral on time so that you have the opportunity to approach the family and offer your condolences. The immediate family will be sitting together, and you can briefly greet all of them and shake their hands before taking your seat. Speak demurely and offer your love and support to the family. There will usually be a line of people waiting to greet the family, so keep comments brief until you have the opportunity to speak with family members after the funeral.

Expressions of Sympathy

Approaching a family member with words of comfort can be a little disconcerting. Certainly, you are wondering what to say and if what you are saying is the right thing. A few sympathetic suggestions include:

- ❧ I am sorry for your loss.
- ❧ I also loved this person and I feel sad too.
- ❧ I know how much the deceased loved and cared for you and his family.
- ❧ The deceased was a wonderful person and I am glad to have known him.
- ❧ I am sorry to hear this sad news.
- ❧ The deceased will be missed greatly.

You do not have to approach the casket to view the body if you are uncomfortable. Instead, proceed to the family to offer your condolences.

Sign the Guest Book

Make sure that you sign the guest book so the family will know who attended the funeral. Also, the guest book makes it easier for the family to mail thank-you cards. With all of the hustle and bustle, the family might forget someone who actually attended and the book will serve as a reminder.

Wear Modest Clothes

Typically a dark suit or dress is worn to a funeral or memorial service. However, even though that rule is not as stringent as it used to be, you're never dressed inappropriately when in a dark suit or dress.

What's not appropriate at a funeral is anything party-like and flashy. Skin-tight outfits and low plunging necklines also are inappropriate. Men's hats should be removed in places of worship.

Some traditions require that women dress very modestly. If you are unsure of the tradition, ask someone who will know what tradition calls for. If you do not have the opportunity to ask someone, play it safe and make sure that your dress or skirt falls below the knee and your arms and cleavage are entirely covered.

Send Flowers

Out-of-town relatives and friends who are unable to attend the services may send flowers and words of condolence to the house of worship, the funeral home, or the family home. If you decide to send flowers or a plant to the funeral home, schedule them to arrive before public calling hours will begin. Sometimes families ask that donations be made to charitable organizations in lieu of flowers. When that is the case, you should follow their wishes.

Taking Video and Photos

Videotaping typically should not be done at a funeral. If someone wants to tape the service, only the eulogies should be taped, and even then only with the consent of the family. Photos should not be taken unless the funeral is that of someone very prestigious or prominent and the family has granted permission.

Memorial Services

A memorial service can be held in addition to a funeral or even take the place of a funeral, although it can be held weeks or months after the death. Sometimes a memorial service is held when the deceased has several family or friends that could not attend the service. The major difference between a memorial service and a funeral is the absence of the body. Instead, photos of the deceased may be enlarged and placed in the front of the venue. The order of service can stay the same even though the venue could be at a church, public garden, or even someone's home.

While funerals usually are held by the family of the deceased, memorial services can be held at the request of the family, friends, or even organizations to which the deceased belonged. Often, if a beloved professor dies, his students might organize a memorial service so that other students from out of town who were unable to attend the funeral can pay their respects.

When you have a close friend or family member who passes away, the responsibility may fall on you to make the arrangements. This section gives a general overview of the etiquette details as a small way to make your difficult job a bit easier.

Notices of the Death

When someone dies, usually a notice is printed in the local newspapers. Contact local newspapers to find out the process for submitting death notices. If the deceased lived in another city prior to his or her death, notices can be made there as well, particularly in his or her hometown. When preparing a notice or obituary, include the following information:

- Name of the deceased
- Date and place where he or she died
- Cause of death (optional and up to your family)
- Name of spouse
- City and date of birth
- Company where the person was employed
- Education, military service, or other distinguished awards
- Names of survivors and their relationship to the deceased
- Information about the funeral and memorial service including location, date, and time
- Address where to send donations

Asking Friends to Participate in the Services

When you ask a friend of the deceased to participate in the funeral service, it is a great honor. You should be very clear and explain exactly what is needed. If you want this friend to read a certain a scripture, poem, or to give a eulogy, you should make the request very clear and even advise where in the program the person can participate.

If someone asks you to take part in a loved one's funeral or memorial, make sure you are very clear on what is expected of you. If you are asked to convey a special memory about the deceased, you should write down a few notes so that you don't forget any special highlights. This is the time to honor the deceased, and you want to be sure that you don't leave anything pertinent out of your remarks.

If, however, you feel that you can't participate without getting too emotional, explain to the family or friend why you don't think you can accept the request, but still make it known that you realize being asked to participate is a special honor.

cal says ...

If you ask a friend or loved one of your deceased family member to take part in the funeral, be sure to tell the person that you understand if he cannot or does not want to participate. Speaking in public or serving as a pallbearer are very emotional experiences, and not everyone may want to oblige your request.

General Etiquette for the Funeral

Funerals are usually held in a place of worship with a burial following shortly after. The family is generally seated together and in the front of the venue where the funeral is held. If the deceased had a long-term mate, or spouse equivalent, he or she should be seated with the family. The mate should be acknowledged on the obituary if the deceased has requested that this person be treated as family.

After the burial, family members and those who attended the funeral often get together at a place of worship, restaurant, or family member's home to share a meal. After the funeral and burial, the mood is often lighter and people may recall the deceased and share fond moments with the family. Often, family and friends will share a good laugh, which is appropriate in that setting. After the services, life for the family continues, which is when they will need company and kind words as the healing process begins.

AVOID FUNERAL FAUX PAS

- ∾ During a time of grief, a family needs as much love and support as possible. The last thing the family needs is to have to navigate family drama while planning the service and the funeral. Friends and family should remember that and be as courteous as possible.

- ∾ Former spouses should not sit with the family unless invited. Instead, the former spouse should sit in another part of the sanctuary

- All children of the deceased should sit with the family, even if the deceased was divorced.
- Those who were engaged in an extramarital affair with the deceased should not attend the funeral.

Funeral Thank-You Notes

Even though a funeral is a sad and stressful time, thank-you notes should be sent to those who supported you during your time of need, including those who attended the funeral or who gave flowers or plants, contributions, or personal services and their time, including participating in the service. The rules are changing and all of the acknowledgements don't have to be handwritten. Instead a printed card that expresses thanks can be mailed. The card can read something like this:

> The family of Samuel David Burns thanks you for your support and kindness in our time of sorrow.

A few handwritten lines along with the printed card is an acceptable acknowledgment. For the family and friends who were especially helpful, a handwritten note should be sent. In this instance, a few lines are adequate.

conclusion

Etiquette, or being polite, considerate, and even compassionate, is something that everyone should incorporate in all aspects of life. Whether you—or someone else—is dining, texting, dating, or grieving, consideration always is appreciated.

Etiquette is not about being stuffy or prudish. It's a way of life that, when used, makes us all better people. Etiquette is showing appreciation by writing thank-you letters; it's about showing respect when participating in a religious ceremony—even if it's not your religion—and it's about saying "excuse me," "I'm sorry," or even "no, thank you." As our mothers say, it's about "how to *be*." Classy, elegant, and, above all, ladylike.

index

Adoptive families, showers
    for, 145
Allergies, guests with, 101

Baby showers, 135–46
    gifts and favors, 139,
        141, 152
    guest list/invitations,
        137–38
    menu/decorations/
        games, 139–41
    special circumstances,
        143–45
    themes, 141–42

Dating
    online, 180, 182
    in workplace, 162–63
Dining out, 1–22. *See also*
    Tricky foods; Wine
    being seated and
        ordering, 5–11
    handling bill, 4–5
    styles of dining, 18–20

table manners, 12–13
table setting basics,
    14–18, 20–22, 33–34
tipping, 42–43

E-mail, 172–79
Engagement
    announcement,
    114–16

Funerals, 201–13
    general etiquette,
    206–13
    helping with
        preparations, 204–6

Gifts
    art of giving, 147–56
    baby shower, 139, 141,
        152
    hostess, 109, 191,
        192–95
    wedding, 125–28
    workplace, 151–52

Guests, at weddings
    invitations for,
        121–24
    making list of, 120–21
    responsibilities of, 128,
        130–32
Guests, in home
    being good guest,
        186–95
    preparing to be hostess,
        195–200

Interview, for new job,
    167–68
Introductions and
    mingling, 53–65
    basic rules of, 56–63
Invitations
    baby shower, 137
    party, 92–95
    wedding, 121–24

Obituaries, 210
Outdoor parties, 103–5

Parties and entertaining,
87–110
invitations, 92–95
planning, 95–105
special situations,
105–10
types of parties, 90–92

Resume, 166–67

Sexual harassment, 164
Sympathy, ways to express,
207

Table manners, 12–13
Table setting basics, 14–18,
20–22, 33–34
Technology, 171–84
BlackBerry devices,
184
cell phones, 182–84
e-mail, 172–79
online dating, 180, 182
social networking,
179–80
Thank-you notes
after funeral, 213
after stay as guest,
191–92
for gifts, 128, 156

Tipping, 39–52
at beauty salons,
45–46
general guidelines,
46–52
in hotels, 44–45
in restaurants and bars,
44–45
Tricky foods, 67–86
appetizers, 69–72
bones, 77–78
desserts, 85–86
fruits, 78–80
hands-on foods, 80–83
main courses, 73–77
spreads/sauces/sides,
83–85

Weddings, 111–34
announcing
engagement,
114–16
bridal party selection,
117–20
expenses of, 116–17
guest list for, 120–21
guests' responsibilities
at, 128, 130–32
invitations for, 121–24
receiving line, 126–27

registering for gifts,
125–26
special situations,
133–34
Wine, 23–28
descriptions of, 26–27
glasses for, 15–16, 33–34
how to serve, 33–35
selecting in restaurant,
10, 35–38
tipping and, 43
types of, 28–32
Workplace issues, 157–70
dating, 162–63
dress code, 163
gift-giving, 151–52
job change/loss, 165–70
office parties, 161–62
personal life and,
158–60
sexual harassment and,
164